THE LEA VALLEY
WALK

THE LEA VALLEY WALK

by

LEIGH HATTS

CICERONE PRESS
2 POLICE SQUARE, MILNTHORPE
CUMBRIA, LA7 7PY
www.cicerone.co.uk

© Lee Valley Park Authority 2001
ISBN   1 85284 313 6

Photographs: Finn Butler, Design Research Unit, except cover photo
(Kingfisher), Les Borg
Maps: Martin Collins

A catalogue record for this book is available from the British Library

Lee Valley Park Information Centre
Abbey Gardens, Waltham Abbey, Essex EN9 1XQ
Information line: 01992 702200
www.leevalleypark.org.uk

ACKNOWLEDGEMENTS
The author is grateful for help and advice from Patience
Bagenal, Richard Durack, Dr Jim Lewis, Marion Marples,
James Hatts, Janet Richardson, Lesley Thirlwell, Richard
Thomas, Trevor Tweent, Cllr John Wing and county librarians
at Hertford, Hoddesdon, Luton and Ware.

Advice to Readers

Readers are advised that while every effort is taken by the
author to ensure the accuracy of this guidebook, changes
can occur which may affect the contents. It is advisable to
check locally on transport, accommodation, shops, etc, but
even rights of way can be altered.

The publisher would welcome notes of any such changes.

Cicerone guidebooks by the same author:
The Thames Path

Front cover: (Main picture) New River; (small pictures, l–r) Lee Valley
Park; Kingfisher; Waltham Abbey

Contents

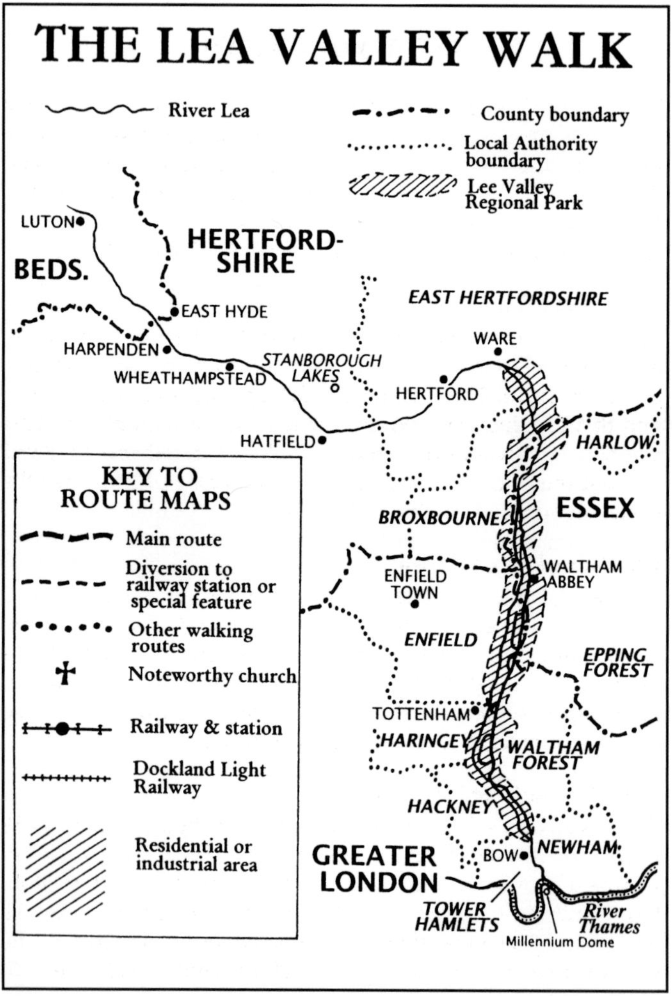
THE LEA VALLEY WALK
River Lea
County boundary
Local Authority boundary
Lee Valley Regional Park
LUTON
BEDS.
HERTFORD-SHIRE
EAST HYDE
EAST HERTFORDSHIRE
HARPENDEN
WHEATHAMPSTEAD
STANBOROUGH LAKES
WARE
HERTFORD
HATFIELD
HARLOW
KEY TO ROUTE MAPS
Main route
Diversion to railway station or special feature
Other walking routes
Noteworthy church
Railway & station
Dockland Light Railway
Residential or industrial area
BROXBOURNE
ESSEX
WALTHAM ABBEY
ENFIELD TOWN
ENFIELD
EPPING FOREST
TOTTENHAM
HARINGEY
WALTHAM FOREST
HACKNEY
GREATER LONDON
BOW
NEWHAM
TOWER HAMLETS
River Thames
Millennium Dome

INTRODUCTION

The Prince of Wales, making his maiden speech in the House of Lords in 1974, described the Lee Valley Park as 'a classic example of what could be done with derelict land if impetus and determination was there'. A quarter of a century later the Lea Valley, once London's market garden, is again recognised as a rich green lung running down the east side of the capital.

Lea or Lee

There are at least 25 different spellings for the river's name. In addition to *Lee* and *Lea* past documents record *Lay, Ley, Leye, Lyge* and even *Lyzan*. The spelling by 1520 appears to have been *Lee*, and this spelling was adopted for acts of parliament. Now the valley is usually known as the *Lea Valley*, as the river is the *River Lea*, but the canal stretch is the *Lee Navigation*, which forms the backbone of the *Lee Valley Regional Park*.

Lee Valley Regional Park

The Lee Valley Park, established by act of parliament in 1967 and Britain's first Regional Park, stretches 26 miles (41km) from Ware in Hertfordshire to the River Thames in London. The Park has become a unique blend of countryside, nature reserves, urban green spaces, heritage sites and sports facilities, and also embraces almost 1000 hectares of open water.

River Lea and Lee Navigation

The River Lea, which rises at Leagrave in Bedfordshire, is 58 miles (98km) long, with much of its last 27 miles (43km) from Hertford canalised from 1767 by engineer John Smeaton. Occasionally the navigation leaves the river to follow Smeaton's new channels, so that there can be meandering stretches of the Old River Lea flowing nearby. Most of the navigation falls within the Lee Valley Regional Park.

Lea Valley Walk

The Lea Valley Walk from Leagrave to Bow in East London was first launched in 1993. The Waltham Abbey to Bow section has been awarded the London Walking Forum kitemark, confirming its status as a fully accessible and comprehensively waymarked route.

Now, with the publication of this guide, the Walk is both being improved higher up the river and extended south to the confluence of the Lea with the Thames, opposite the Millennium Dome.

Millennium Walk

The Lea Valley Walk can be claimed as the Millennium Walk – for half the route, from St Margarets to the Dome, is also a crucial stretch of the 260 mile (439km) Meridian Way. This new route will by 2005 link Cleethorpes in Yorkshire with Peacehaven in Sussex. Eventually the Way will extend further south through France and Spain.

Wildlife and Farmland

In the summer kingfishers can be seen at the source, in the Park and even at Bow. Over 200 different bird species can be found within the boundaries of the Park, which is a major wintering area for birds, especially bitterns.

In Bedfordshire and Hertfordshire the way is through fields with cattle and between paddocks. The Park's water meadows at Waltham Abbey are a dragonfly sanctuary.

The Valley and English History

The Valley, once the boundary between the land ruled by Alfred the Great and Danelaw to the north, has been the setting for many landmark events in England's history. Christian culture emerged from Hertford when the first national church synod united the Celtic and new Roman Christian traditions. King Harold came to Waltham Abbey in 1066 prior to the Battle of Hastings, and his subsequent burial there marked the end of the Saxon era and the beginning of the new dynasty and the Norman influence.

Another dramatic change of dynasty came in 1603 when the Tudor line gave way to the Scottish Stuarts. James VI of Scotland entered London by way of the Lea Valley, pausing near Cheshunt to form his English government. He also brought with him golf, which now flourishes in the Valley.

Earlier, the traumatic Reformation had begun at Waltham Abbey when the worried Henry VIII met the future Archbishop Cranmer. Edward VI, Elizabeth I and Charles I all ascended the throne whilst living in the Lea Valley.

Queen Victoria's influential first prime minister, Lord Melbourne, grew up, lived and worked alongside the River Lea at Brocket Park. Later the Queen's least favourite premier, Palmerston, inherited the same house. Her very last first minister was Lord Salisbury, who lived at Hatfield. Balfour, an early 20th-century prime minister, began his education at Hoddesdon.

Architectural Heritage

England's architectural heritage is well represented in the Valley. Early brick mansions are to be found both near the source in Bedfordshire and in the riverside London village of Homerton. Great stately homes, such as those at Luton Hoo and Brocket Park, have enhanced the river by creating great lakes as a backdrop to varied styles of building visited by royalty and other famous figures. There are also castles, ancient pubs and at Ware the unique gazebos. Rye House Gatehouse near Hoddesdon is a fine example of early English brickwork.

Above all there are the many churches – from Saxon foundations and the ancient Norman Waltham Abbey to the unusual 19th-century brick building at East Hyde.

Literary Heritage

In the Lea Valley three great hymn writers, including William Cowper, composed now famous hymns, and authors such as Trollope and Beatrix Potter also found inspiration here. Isaak Walton's *Compleat Angler* is a tribute to the River Lea, which his contemporary John Stow described as 'a pleasant and useful river'.

Up and Down the Valley

On the Lea Valley Walk one will come across familiar names. A 20th-century descendant of 15th-century Lord Wenlock, associated with Luton Church and at Someries Castle, is commemorated at Sutton House in Homerton. Meanwhile, Sir Ralph Sadleir's daughter moved upstream and entertained Queen Elizabeth I at Stanstead Abbotts. The Cecils, who presided at Theobalds under the Tudors, moved upstream to Hatfield under the Stuarts, leaving their old house for the King to use as his Lea Valley residence.

Moving down the river, the Brocket family is associated with Wheathampstead, Lemsford and Hatfield.

The valley has long been a green corridor for people on foot, horseback and water. The Romans built Ermine Street, and the Danes rowed up the river in 854. The last horse-drawn barge passed along the canal in the mid-1950s and now the towpath is part of the the walking route into London linking the ancient Icknield Way with the Thames Path.

Maps

The recommended maps, in addition to those in this book, are the Ordnance Survey Explorer maps. Also useful is the OS Herts Street Atlas (Philips, £5.99), which also covers Luton. South of Waltham Abbey many of the London street maps can be helpful.

Transport

The Walk has been divided into sections according to the many handy railway stations along the route. Some display the Lea Valley Walk swan symbol signs waymarking the route from the station to the Walk. Rail information is available on 08457 484950.

Enjoying the Walk

This is a walk that can be enjoyed by everybody from the keen long-distance walker to those with young children or those new to taking exercise. Thanks to the many railway stations alongside the Park, between Ware and London, the Walk can be reached easily. Some of the sections are very short. Indeed, these stretches

The farmhouse near Someries Castle where Joseph Conrad wrote Under Western Eyes

often contain much heritage and countryside to enjoy – such as the one mile between Cheshunt and Waltham Abbey.

Refreshment is an important part of any walk, and details of pubs and cafés have been included. However, it is often sensible to carry a drink. Water, frozen overnight (do not fill the bottle to the top), remains cool long into a hot day.

Country Code

Visitors to the countryside should close any already shut gates behind them and not stray from paths. Livestock should be treated with respect and dogs kept under close control near farm animals.

Healthy Walking

Walking is not only enjoyable but also a healthy activity that can even extend life. The Lea Valley Walk is the Millennium exercise route full of heritage, wildlife and opportunity.

1. Leagrave to Luton

Leagrave Station (Thameslink) to Luton Station (Thameslink and Midland Mainline)

Maps:	**1–2**
Distance:	**4 miles (6.5km)**
OS Map:	**OS Explorer 193 (Luton and Stevenage)**

Once the River Lea had enough water just beyond the source to drive a mill. But this first stretch into Luton is remarkably rural, with rare plants and the possibility of seeing a kingfisher. The first pub on the river is Bedfordshire's oldest building.

LEAGRAVE ROUNDABOUT features the Three Horseshoes sign from the pub which once stood on the site of McDonald's. The area grew slowly during the 20th century with industry and housing. In Leagrave High Street (west of the station) there is St Luke's Church which dates only from 1956 but is known for its rare Norman Blamey mural.

To reach the start of the Lea Valley Walk: Turn right out of Leagrave Station booking office and walk down the hill. Go right into Grange Avenue and under the railway to reach a roundabout. Go left to walk up Sundon Road. (The safest route here is to briefly go right to cross the end of Marsh Road to McDonald's. Bear left to cross the end of Bramingham Road and continue into Sundon Road with the traffic to the left.)

Keeping the traffic to the left and Leagrave Common to the right walk as far as the next road junction. Here cross Houghton Brook and at once go right into the park. Beyond the building pass a footbridge and keep ahead along the side of the playing field. Where the stream veers away keep forward along the edge

MAP 1

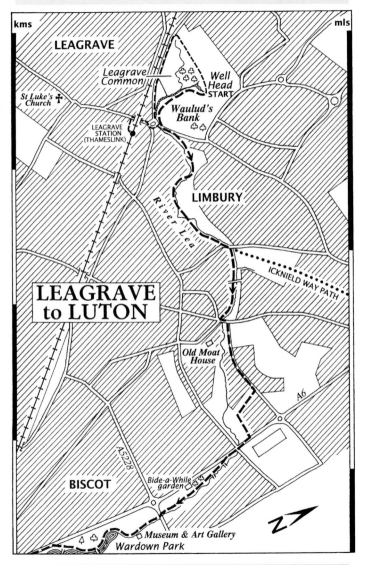

kms

mls

LEAGRAVE

Leagrave Common

Well Head START

St Luke's Church

Waulud's Bank

LEAGRAVE STATION (THAMESLINK)

River Lea

LIMBURY

ICKNIELD WAY PATH

LEAGRAVE to LUTON

Old Moat House

A6

A5228

BISCOT

Bide-a-While garden

Museum & Art Gallery
Wardown Park

N

of a wood, Rotten Spinney (right). After the ground rises onto ancient Waulud's Bank the track meets a metalled path at a T-junction. Turn right to find a concrete platform over a grating giving a view down the infant River Lea. This point, known as Well Head, is the official start of the Lea Valley Walk.

WELL HEAD and START OF WALK The concrete platform covers a storm-water outflow. The river's source is the Five Springs between here and the point where the channel bends south. One spring is on the left bank but not now identifiable. The first two on the right bank can be found amongst the watercress, where in the early part of the year there is often a visible bubbling of water in addition to the continuous flow. Here and on the downstream marsh 220 plant species have been recorded, including rushes, marsh marigold and even a rare watercress. Kingfishers can be spotted and even an occasional heron. Where Houghton Brook, the Lea's first tributary, joins water voles can be found. The Five Springs are in a corner of the 4000-year-old Waulud's Bank, a Neolithic site which may have been used for gatherings or as a worship centre. Flint tools found on this site, a henge as old as Stonehenge, are displayed in Luton Museum (see 'Wardown Park' below).

Cross the top of the outflow and follow the metalled path near the river (right). To the left is the main area of Waulud's Bank. Soon the path passes between a bridge (right) and Marsh House.

MARSH HOUSE, now a community centre, is the former farmhouse of Marsh Farm. Waulud's Bank, where there is now an annual haycut, was cultivated well into the 20th century and cattle grazed on the marsh. Earlier the Common, which extended further west beyond the railway, was a recreation area for Luton and known as both 'Leagrave-on-Sea' and the 'Blockers' Seaside' – after the hat-industry workers who made the wooden blocks (see 'Luton', Walk 2). Here the footbridge spans a River Lea now made wider by a second tributary, Lewsey Brook. (A further bridge, over the brook, leads to restored marshland.)

Keep forward with the Lea (right) to a road by the roundabout and McDonald's to join the Icknield Way Trail.

ICKNIELD WAY The beginning of the Lea Valley Walk shares the way with the Icknield Way Trail, a 105 mile (169km) regional route based closely on the line of Britain's oldest road, which passes the ancient Waulud's Bank by the river's source. The Icknield Way runs from nearby Ivinghoe Beacon to Thetford in Norfolk. The path also continues to the south-west as The Ridgeway national trail to Overton Hill, near Avebury in Wiltshire. Leaflets are available from Countryside Agency, Ortona House, 110 Hills Road, Cambridge CB2 1LQ. *The Icknield Way Path: A Guide for Horseriders, Cyclists and Others* is available from East Anglian Trails, Pip's Peace, Kenton, Stowmarket IP14 6JS (£4.50 including postage), and *The Icknield Way Path: A Walkers' Guide* is available from Icknield Way Association, 19 Boundary Road, Bishops Stortford CM23 5LE (£5.50 including postage).

Cross the end of Bramingham Road (by McDonald's) and turn left to pass over the river. After a short distance bear right onto a metalled path running parallel to the Lea. Where the path divides go right to cross the bridge. The river is now to the left, but as it bends again, cross the next two bridges.

On reaching Neville Road (number 70 is opposite) turn left to the bridge at Limbury, where the road changes its name to Icknield Way – although the Icknield Way Trail turns right with the Lea Valley Walk. So turn right before the bridge to continue on a floodbank, with the Lea to the left, and pass a footbridge which is the site of Limbury Mill.

LIMBURY MILL SITE There was a mill on this site from Saxon times until the end of the 14th century. Here the Icknield Way leaves the Lea Valley Walk.

After the Cats Brook joins from the far side, the path crosses Runfold Avenue and continues ahead to reach Bancroft Road at Biscot.

Half-right, and a few yards down Nunnery Lane, is the Old Moat House pub.

OLD MOAT HOUSE is a former manor house dating from 1370 and the oldest secular building in the Luton area. Its still filled moat was once fed by the River Lea. Under the thatch, and visible from inside, is a fine timber roof which may have come from a monastic house – giving rise to the lane's name. John Acworth, who was living here in 1500 and about the time the new roof was put on, is commemorated in Luton Church (see 'St Mary's, Luton', Walk 2). A plaque on the pub's ground floor records a very heavy hailstorm in 1666. The restoration and conversion to a pub took place in 1969.

At Bancroft Road the Walk continues left over the river and right along Riddy Lane. Just beyond Broughton Avenue (right) turn right up a wide grassed area – a late Iron Age cemetery. The River Lea is down the slope at the far end, but the Walk turns left on the high ground.

At the main road turn right to cross the river and reach a crossroads. Here cross the main road to continue ahead on the left-hand pavement. The river is now to the left. Walk along the road, but where there is a footbridge (left) bear left across the grass to join the path – keeping the river on the left. Keep forward past the next bridge to find a path following the river through the woodland ahead. Briefly the path passes through a garden, known as Bide-a-While, before the way becomes grassed.

BIDE-A-WHILE is the name of the formal garden in the centre of this long riverside plot once known as Boggs Mead. The southern end was an osier bed into the 20th century for one of the last basket makers in Luton. The garden, given to the public in 1952, has two dawn redwood trees thought to be extinct until rediscovered in China.

At a road cross over and go left for a few yards to find a wooden stile. Beyond the stile keep forward above the terracing up the side of a cricket field. At the far corner go ahead into Wardown Park.

WARDOWN PARK was a farm until 1873, when the house was rebuilt with Luton bricks and the lake created from the River Lea. It became a public park in 1905. The house is now the Luton Museum and Art Gallery, with displays on Waulud's Bank finds (see 'Well Head', above), early Luton and the local hat industry, which even produced straw helmets for the police. Roman gold coins found in Bedfordshire and once belonging to Britain's first millionaires are among recent additions. (Open Tue–Sat 10am–5pm; Sun 2–5pm; free). Waymarks painted on the park paths are for a circular Wardown Walk, promoted as a gentle, one-hour healthy walk.

Walk past the house (left) and round a double bend. At a main path go right and left down to the lake. Keep the water to the left to cross the Lea and walk the length of the lake (left). At the far end the path joins the main road (see Map 2) with the river running on both sides. Here New Bedford Road has the feel of a causeway. Soon, on the right, is the Moor – the green remnant of Great Moor. Keep forward to pass under the railway bridge to enter Luton.

To reach Luton Station (Map 2): Turn left along Mill Street to cross the now united River Lea. The road leads into Station Road.

Refreshments

Leagrave Roundabout: McDonald's; open all day.

Old Moat House: Nunnery Lane, Biscot; Mon–Fri 12–2.30pm and 5.30–11pm; Sat and Sun open all day; meals and bar food.

Accommodation

Wardown Park: Aiken House, 53 Montrose Avenue LU3 1HP; tel. 01582 617379; off Wardown Park roundabout.

See also Luton 'Accommodation' (Walk 2).

2. Luton to Luton Airport Parkway Station

*Luton Station (Thameslink and Midland Mainline) to Luton
Airport Parkway Station (Thameslink)*

Map:	**2**
Distance:	**2 miles (3km)**
OS Maps:	**OS Explorer 193 (Luton and Stevenage) and 182 (St Albans and Hatfield)**

Luton has a remarkable church visited annually for a decade by
the Queen. The building can be seen framed in the window at
the end of the vast indoor shopping centre. Along one side is the
old high street, whilst on the other is the River Lea and the little
streets where the hat industry was once concentrated. This is a
short walk between Luton's two stations – but it can take some
time, as there is much to delay the walker.

LUTON lies in the river valley and is called *Lintone,* meaning
town on the Lea, in the Domesday Book, which records three
watermills here on the Lea. North Mill stood at about the
junction of Mill and Manchester Streets, where the Walk
enters the town centre. Church (or Abbey) Mill was near the
station, and Brache Mill was just south of the recreation
ground in Windmill Road. In Luton the two streams of the
Lea converge to run under Mill Street. There is a brief view
outside the Galaxy centre before the river continues underground as far as Cheapside, where it is behind the buildings
of Guildford and John Streets – the Melson Arms on the
corner suffered from damp cellars until the Lea was diverted
a few feet in the 1960s. The river is again underground along
Church Street. Church Mill was to the east of the churchyard.

By the 15th century brewing and malting were established
thanks to the water of the Lea. The Red Lion on George Street's

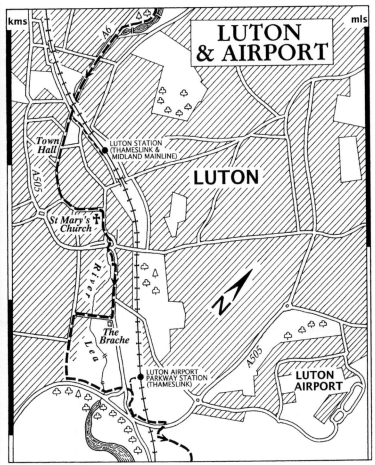

MAP 2

Market Hill dates from 1475 and was one of many coaching inns. In 1781 Dr Johnson could still call Luton a 'village'. By 1840 the east side of George Street had both inns and hat warehouses.

Straw-plaiting to make hats started in the late 18th century and the height of the hat industry here was around 1900, when many of the buildings between the shopping centre and the station were occupied by the trade. Cheap plait from the Far East led to a boom in straw boaters. A hat press machine can be seen on the corner of Bute and Guildford Streets. Luton Town football team is known as the Hatters. The hat industry still exists, but the arrival of Vauxhall Motors in 1905 saw the start of a new industry.

To reach the Walk from Luton Station: Turn right down Station Road into Mill Street and continue to the end.

Go left along Manchester Street passing under a railway bridge to reach the Town Hall.

LUTON TOWN HALL was opened in 1936 after the old one burned down during the 1919 peace celebrations. The 144ft high Portland stone tower was so bright that in the Second World War it had to be shrouded in camouflage.

Continue along the traffic-free George Street. At the far end go left down Church Street to pass Luton Church.

ST MARY'S LUTON, Bedfordshire's largest church, was founded about 1121. Its outstanding feature outside is the flint and stone chequerwork, and inside the 14th-century baptistry. The south door was a gift from Cardinal Wolsey, who was briefly patron of the church. The Wenlock Chapel was built by Lord Wenlock of Someries Castle (see Walk 3). The first stall on the left of the chapel entrance was used by the Queen when she attended morning service during her annual November weekend at Luton Hoo (see Walk 3) as a guest of Sir Harold Wernher, who is commemorated on the north wall. In the north transept there is a brass of John Acworth who lived at the Moat House (see Walk 1).

Turn right with the churchyard and beyond Vicarage Street go down the subway. Here, in the middle of the roundabout, do not be tempted over the River Lea but bear right through another subway. Go left up to pass the MacDonald Humphrey building (right) and turn the corner to find the River Lea emerging on the left. At a road go left to cross the water and then right into Windmill Road. (The Brache Mill once stood near here.) Continue ahead past the Windmill Hill pub (left) and uphill to The Brache pub at the junction with Osborne Road.

Go right to walk down Osborne Road into the valley to cross the river. (From 2001 it should be possible to turn left along the river and avoid Park Street ahead.) At the Park Street junction go left. Just before the flyover and Luton Hoo gates (see Walk 3) turn left along a metalled footpath back to cross the river. After the bridge below the main road the path turns left. Go right under a road. At the far end is Parkway Road leading to Luton Airport Parkway Station (left).

To reach Luton Airport Parkway Station: Turn right and, after a short distance, cross the road to follow the pavement round the corner to the station.

Refreshments

Luton: Many cafés in shopping centre and town.

Luton: The Brache, Osborne Road; open all day; on Walk on southern edge of town.

Accommodation

Luton: Red Lion Hotel, Castle Street LU1 3AA; tel. 01582 413881; part of Brookes Café Bar on Walk in town centre.

Luton: The O'Leary's, 85 Havelock Road LU2 7PP; tel. 01582 618077.

Luton: Hill House, 93 London Road LU1 3RG; tel. 01582 722725.

Luton: Stockwood Hotel, 41–43 Stockwood Crescent LU1 3SS; tel. 01582 721000.

Luton: Aiken House, 53 Montrose Avenue LU3 1HP; tel. 01582 617379; off Wardown Park roundabout.

Luton: The Brache (Travel Inn), Osborne Road LU1 3HJ; tel. 01582 417654; on Walk on southern edge of town; children welcome.

3. Luton Airport Parkway to Harpenden

*Luton Airport Parkway Station (Thameslink) to Harpenden
Station (Thameslink)*

Maps:	2–3
Distance:	4½ miles (7km)
OS Maps:	**OS Explorer 193 (Luton and Stevenage) and 182 (St Albans and Hatfield)**

The way out of Luton is by way of a viewpoint by the airport,
before the Walk passes the first of the valley's several important
stately homes. Later a former railway line provides an easy path
to the edge of Harpenden. An optional early diversion offers the
chance to see the impressive remains of one of England's oldest
brick houses.

LUTON AIRPORT PARKWAY STATION, on the town's
southern edge, was built to serve Luton Airport. Now most
trains stop at both Luton stations.

To reach the Walk: Follow Parkway Road from the station
forecourt. The Walk joins from the right before the end of the
road.

Follow Parkway Road to a roundabout and turn left. Immediately before the flyover go left up a narrow path which climbs up
to steps leading to the high Airport Way road. Turn left along the
pavement. Soon the road crosses high over the railway line.
Where the pavement turns away from the road get ready to cross
the road **with care**. On the far side climb the steps to a stile where
there is a view across Luton by the fence of Luton Airport.

LUTON AIRPORT, which opened in 1939 with Luton-born
future novelist Arthur Hailey present, now handles around 5
million passengers a year – many flying on low-fare services
such as easyJet. Luton Airport Parkway Station and the £40m

MAP 3

terminal, which were both opened by the Queen in 1999, are expected to lead to a further growth in passenger numbers. Yet the surrounding grass-land remains a haven for wild-life such as hares, sky-larks and butterflies.

Go ahead from the stile and turn left with the airport fence to follow the path along the high ground and then down into the valley.

At the bottom of the hill go left only to visit Someries Castle (see below).

The Walk continues to the right following the bottom of the valley. The old track becomes more distinct on approaching two houses. Keep forward under the railway to a road. Opposite is the wall of Luton Hoo.

Turn left along the

road for a short distance to find, on the left, a stile. Once in the field keep near the bank with the road to the right. After a tunnel (left) the ground rises and a handy waymark on a post points the way towards the left side of the field. From here there are occasional glimpses of Luton Hoo mansion (right).

LUTON HOO stands on high ground in the Capability Brown landscaped parkland where the River Lea becomes a 60 acre lake as it passes below. There has been a house on the site since Tudor times, and owners have included Lord Bute, who made changes whilst prime minister in 1763. The Duke of Clarence in 1891 was at Luton Hoo to announce his engagement to Princess May – she later married his brother and became Queen Mary. The present mansion, largely built in 1903 for diamond magnate Sir Julius Wernher, is by Mewès & Davis – French architects of the Ritz. From 1948 until the 1970s it was the home of racehorse owners Sir Harold Wernher and his wife Lady Zia, daughter of Grand Duke Michael Michaelovitch of Russia. For many years the Queen and Prince Philip spent a weekend here every November to celebrate their wedding anniversary with the couple. Princess Alexandra met her husband Angus Ogilvy whilst staying at the house. Sir Harold, who died in 1973, was succeeded by his grandson Nicholas Phillips, who in 1991 was found dead after accumulating debts. In 1999 the house and estate were purchased by Elite Hotels.

At the far end of the very long field go over stiles at a road and continue ahead on a short rising path which soon bears left to join the bed of the former Welwyn–Luton–Dunstable railway line. The wooded path runs as far as a missing bridge, where steps lead down to the road. Turn left for a few metres before crossing the road with care.

A short path leads into the trees. Cross a stile and bear right to find steps leading up to a second stile on top of the former railway embankment. The path crosses high above the River Lea before running alongside a sewage works to a road at New Mill End. Opposite is the pink-washed Luton Hoo Station House.

NEW MILL END Here on the river was the original Saxon-built Stapleford Mill. *New* refers to a successor built in 1400 and worked until the 20th century. Luton Hoo Station closed in 1965 along with the railway line which ran from Dunstable to Welwyn via Luton. This railway line opened in 1858 – ten years ahead of the nearby Midland main line. The Prince of Wales, the future Edward VII, used the station (now a private house) at least twice when visiting Luton Hoo's mansion, reached by way of the gateway opposite.

Continue over the stile by the gateway to the left of the Station House. The platform can be seen to the right through the under-growth. The path is wooded as it runs past more Thames Water sewage works. For a short time the flat surface of the railway bed is lost. Later the way meets the mainline Luton–London railway. Do not go under the bridge but, just before, go right up steps to follow the side of the embankment (left). There is a huge field to the right. On meeting an open road go left under the railway bridge and follow Thrales End Lane, part of the Chiltern Way, down towards East Hyde. The Walk turns right up onto the old railway just before the river.

EAST HYDE bridge is the boundary between Bedfordshire upstream and Hertfordshire. The hamlet has a remarkable Romanesque-style church built in 1840. Architect Benjamin Ferrey was inspired by Canterbury Cathedral's Norman guest house. Behind the church, at the top of the sloping churchyard, is the Wernher mausoleum, resembling the medieval shrine tomb of St Alban at St Albans. There has been a mill at downstream Hyde Mill Farm since Norman times. The Chiltern Way is a 215km walk round the Chilterns from Ewelme in the west to Hollybush Hill near Great Offley in the east. A guide (£7.90) is available from the Chiltern Society (tel. 01923 446960).

The Walk now leaves Bedfordshire to enter Hertfordshire by continuing along the wooded old railway embankment with the river to the left. After a short distance there is a clearing and a seat with a view over the valley to Hyde Mill Farm.

The path runs along the side of the field with the river screened by trees (left) and the railway over to the right. At the far end go through a kissing gate and soon the way becomes a shady sunken path. A slope leads up to a road at Cold Harbour on the edge of Harpenden. To the left, near the river, is the Red Cow.

> **COLD HARBOUR** Traffic had to use a ford here until as late as 1964, when a bridge was built. The Red Cow has been a pub since 1851 and for a time in the 19th century had a small grocer's shop attached.

Cross the narrow dual carriageway to follow the track bed between gardens of houses. Do not go forward to a residential road but bear left and left again at a T-junction to reach the main road opposite Batford's Pickford Bridge.

Go right and cross the road to go into the car park just beyond the modern church. Go through the kissing gate and follow the grass path as far as a long bridge over the stream and river.

To reach the Harpenden Station: Turn right along the metalled footpath up to cross Marquis Lane and reach the Post Office and Station Rd Stores on the bend of Station Road. Continue past the shop and up the hill. Go under the railway bridge and turn left to the station.

Refreshments
Cold Harbour (near Harpenden): Red Cow; open all day.

Accommodation
See 'Accommodation', Walk 2.

Diversion to Someries Castle
At the bottom of the hill turn left to stay with the airport fence. The path runs along the field boundary which climbs and bears south-east round to the right. After a grove of trees (left) there is a hedge. Go over the gate on the left and bear half-right to pass between the brick Someries Castle (right) and the farmhouse. Go

over the stile by the gate and turn immediately right to find the gate leading into the castle grounds.

SOMERIES CASTLE is named after the Someries family, who lived in a house on a site just visible to the west. The ruined building, which includes a gateway, porter's lodge and part of a chapel, is the remains of the earliest house in Bedfordshire to be built of brick. Its first occupant may have been Lord Wenlock, who died at the Battle of Tewkesbury in 1471. Then the building, along with the Manor of Luton, was granted to Thomas Rotherham, Bishop of Lincoln, who later became Cardinal Archbishop of York. The castle was dismantled in the 1740s, when the bricks were used to improve the next door farm buildings, including the farmhouse where Joseph Conrad wrote his novel *Under Western Eyes*. His guests included fellow author Ford Madox Ford, and here in 1908 they sorted through contributions by John Galsworthy, Thomas Hardy, Henry James and H.G. Wells to create the first issue of *The English Review*. The Queen once joined a shooting party here during one of her visits to Luton Hoo (see above). In the 1950s cows were known to stray onto the runway of the nearby airport.

4. Harpenden to Hatfield

Harpenden Station (Thameslink) to Hatfield Station
(WAGN Railway)

Maps:	3–5
Distance:	**8 miles (13km)**
OS Map:	**OS Explorer 182 (St Albans and Hatfield)**

Here, just inside Hertfordshire, the Walk soon leaves the old railway to go up to a viewpoint over Wheathampstead, which has a unique church spire rising above a church little changed for 650 years. The next landmark is Brocket Park's mansion and lake. Beyond the riverside village of Lemsford comes the modern Stanborough Park with its massive man-made lakes fashioned for the residents of Welwyn Garden City. But on the edge of Hatfield the Lea still turns a working flour mill.

HARPENDEN is usually called a village, although there are several supermarkets discreetly placed behind the High Street where the Common pleasantly impinges. St Nicholas Church, although rebuilt in 1862, retains its 15th-century tower and some early monuments. Buried in the churchyard (west side in line with nesting box on tree) is Count de Voilemont – the real guilty party in the Captain Dreyfus affair. In 1984 the church was the scene of local resident Eric Morecambe's funeral. Behind the Harpenden Arms there is a medieval hall house (2 Southdown Road). Further along the Common's east side is 16th-century Harpenden Hall and almshouses. The Statty Fair is held every September on the Common. Actress Ellen Terry (1847–1928) brought up her son designer Gordon Craig here whilst enjoying a rural life keeping ducks and chickens. A wheel came off her trap when she left the house to avoid creditors, but fortunately a passing huntsman turned out to be dramatist Charles Reade,

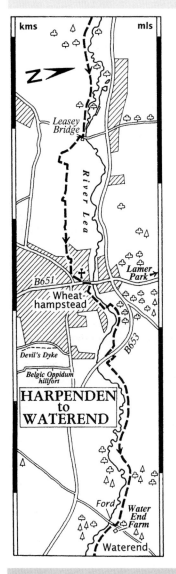

MAP 4

who offered her a leading part in a play.

BATFORD is the name of the riverside community in the valley on the eastern edge of Harpenden. All Saints Church in Station Road opened in 1965 as a successor to a church in Coldharbour Lane. Waveney Road, to the west of the bridge, marks the site of Harpenden East Station, which closed in 1965 and where manure arrived daily from London Zoo for a nursery. The nearby Pickford Bridge was a main crossing for many years, with Pickford Mill producing flour until 1897. The river between here and downstream Batford Mill was rich in watercress beds until 1947, but the falling water-table makes restoration difficult. However, the weirs were repaired in the 1970s by the Upper Lea Valley Group. Charles Lamb knew this area, and in *Essays on Elia* there is mention of Mackerye End, east of the river, which he visited as a child.

To reach the Walk: Turn right out of Harpenden Station and go right under the railway bridge to follow Station Road uphill and down to Batford. On reaching the Post Office and Station Rd Stores at the bottom of the hill go ahead over Marquis Lane and down the metalled path. The River Lea is ahead at the footbridge.

At the footbridge turn right along the riverbank, with the water on the left. Soon there is a view of the divided river joining at the weir. Further downstream there is Batford Mill footbridge and ford. The old mill building can be seen by crossing the bridge.

> **BATFORD MILL**, built as a flour mill in 1860, turned to grinding bones for fertilizer from 1932 until 1950. The nearby Marquis of Granby pub has had its present name since 1799. Earlier, when owned by the mill, it was known as the Swan. A little further downstream an osier bed was planted as late as 1927 for basket-making.

Do not cross the river but go right up Crabtree Lane to turn left into Marquis Lane at the Marquis of Granby. At the line of houses walk on the pavement and at the end go into the wood. Bear right to go up steps to rejoin the former railway line. Turn left and soon the wide way is across a bridge. Coppicing here has encouraged wild flowers. After ¾ mile (1km) the path reaches the former level crossing at Leasey Bridge. Opposite is the Gate House.

Turn right up Leasey Bridge Lane for a very short distance before going left up the drive of Little Croft to find a stile on the right. Bear half-left up the sloping field to cross another stile. Stay by the hedge (right) and, having crossed a stile by a gate, go left. Beyond stables (right) the way is enclosed as it runs gently downhill. After a double bend the path continues to be fenced until it climbs gently uphill to pass a seat facing the valley view (left). At the far end go through a kissing gate and left towards a gate. But before the gate bear right to continue in the easterly direction along the side of the field. The way is downhill and again up to pass another viewpoint seat. After a kissing gate keep forward across a field towards Wheathampstead. On the far side the path is alongside back gardens (left) before becoming metalled and following a double bend to a residential road called High Meads. Turn left and right downhill (past Ash Grove, left) towards the Old School with its bell tower. At the bottom turn left past the pillar box to go left into Wheathampstead's churchyard.

WHEATHAMPSTEAD was a settlement in at least 80BC when a Belgic tribe, the Catuvellauni, invaded – hence the hillfort above Devil's Dyke excavated by Sir Mortimer Wheeler. An early visitor was Julius Caesar, who defeated the tribe. The name *Wheathampstead* comes from the Saxon *Hwaethamstede,* meaning house on the wet marsh. The railway was shut under the Beeching cuts so the Railway Hotel became the Abbot John before finally closing. He was born here, and later served as Abbot of nearby St Albans Abbey for thirty years until his death in 1465. His parents, Hugo and Margaret Bostock, are commemorated in brasses in the ancient church – look under the pink carpet in the north transept. They knew this church, which was completed in 1340, though its unusual spire (likened to an upturned ice cream cornet and admired by John Betjeman) was added more recently in 1865. Also in the north transept is a memorial to Apsley Cherry-Garrard, who found Captain Scott's body in the Antarctic. The Garrard family was at Lamer Park to the north for 400 years until 1948. The Jacobean pulpit comes from the Park's chapel, pulled down after a fire. In the south transept, where there is evidence of the Saxon building, is the 16th-century tomb of Sir John Brocket, who lived at Wheathampstead Place opposite the mill in the High Street. The riverside Bull dates from at least 1717.

After passing the church (left) follow the path to the churchyard's far corner. Pass through the narrow gateway and turn right to the road. Go left along the High Street and at the Bull turn right down East Lane. Where East Lane turns away to the right keep ahead on Meads Lane to reach a grassed area. Go over the bridge and ahead to a junction. Turn right and go through all the gateways to reach a lane. Turn left to go under a bridge, and at once go right up steps and bear right along a fenced way. Beyond a stile turn left across a field. On the far side pass a field corner, and before the end go through a kissing gate on the right, before continuing in the same direction.

Follow the wide sweep of grass by the meandering river (right). After a kissing gate the river is lost over to the right as the path runs below a bank. Soon the way becomes grassed and later runs into a wood where the river makes a brief reappearance. Keep forward at a junction and, shortly after a gate, meet a lane at Waterend. Opposite is Water End Farm.

WATER END FARM The house was built in 1610 for the grandfather of Sarah Jennings, who as Countess of Marlborough became a powerful member of Queen Anne's court. Sarah was born at the house in 1660, and it is widely believed that she and the young Princess Anne played here together as children. Of Sarah's many houses only Water End and Blenheim Palace remain unchanged. The lane is on the line of a Roman road from Braughing – a Roman town and the junction for traffic passing between East Anglia and Verulamium (St Albans).

Turn right down the lane to a ford. Just before the water go left along a path. As the river disappears the way is along the bottom of two fields with a fir wood on the hill to the left. There is a brief glimpse of the river (right) before the now narrow path meets a junction on the edge of the Brocket Estate.

Go ahead up the steep wooded hill. The path emerges onto a golf course. Keep forward and, just beyond a building, the path is by a fence (right). Here there is a view of The Broadwater, Brocket Park's lake fed by the River Lea, beyond Brocket Hall.

BROCKET HALL There was a house here in 1239. Today's mansion, designed by James Paine for the Lamb family, was completed in 1780. The bookshelves are by Chippendale and the ceilings by Cipriani. This was the childhood home of William Lamb, the second Lord Melbourne, who was Queen Victoria's first prime minister. The young Queen came here just before his resignation following the 1841 general elec-

The River Lea near its source at Leagrave

The Wernher mausoleum in East Hyde churchyard

MAP 5

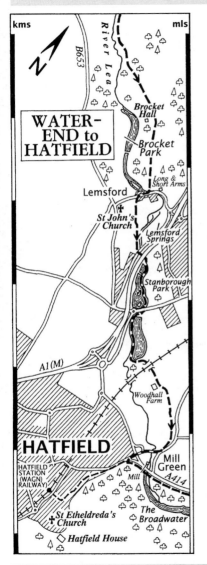

tion. His wife was Byron's admirer Lady Caroline Lamb, who had herself served naked from a giant soup tureen in the dining room at Melbourne's birthday party. On his death here in 1848 the house passed to his sister Emily, whose husband, Lord Palmerston, had been foreign secretary in Melbourne's administration. Palmerston also twice became prime minister and died here but, unlike his brother-in-law, who is buried at Hatfield, Palmerston lies in Westminster Abbey. It is believed that the waltz was introduced to England in the Brocket ballroom. The house passed to the Cowpers of Panshanger Park (page 43). Having been rented by Lord Mountstephen, first president of the Canadian Pacific Railway, from 1892 until his death in 1921, the estate was bought by Sir Charles Nall-Cain Brocket, who became the first Lord Brocket in 1933 and married Ann Page of Fanhams Hall at downstream Ware (Walk 7). In 1981 the third Lord Brocket turned the house into a conference centre, which was the venue for several government summits attended by Presidents Gorbachev, Reagan and Bush. Brocket Hall is now a hotel and conference centre following the third Lord Brocket's conviction in 1996 for a £4.5m insurance fraud involving classic cars once rumoured to have been dumped in the lake. The house reverts to the family in 2056.

As the path meets the drive cross over (right) to climb a stile and follow a sunken way to meet another drive.

(To view the lake and house from the bridge turn right. At the bridge a signpost indicates a path to Lemsford Mill where the Lea Valley Walk can be rejoined.)

The main Walk continues ahead over the golf course. The path then runs by a wood (left) to reach Lemsford by way of a modern bridge at Lemsford Mill.

LEMSFORD Elizabeth I described Lemsford as 'the prettiest village in England'. Until the 17th century the village street was part of Great North Road. The mill and Mill House were built in 1863 and feature in composer J.P Skelly's music-hall song: 'There's an old mill by the stream, Nellie Dean/Where we used to sit and dream, Nellie Dean'. Skelly came across the mill whilst staying at Brocket Hall and by the end of the century the song was popular with Boer War troops. The Long and Short Arm Inn (rebuilt, but dating from 1734) maintained, on the new main road to the north, a wooden signal with two arms indicating the water level at the ford to encourage stage coaches into the village. In 1875 Joseph Arch's Agricultural Labourers' Union preferred to meet at the Sun Inn, which kept cows and chickens and sold milk as well as beer. From here the River Lea is boosted by the Lemsford Springs after the river bends south. St John's Church, which stands alone to the west at Brocket Corner, dates from as recently as 1858, when the parish was created. The church was built on the death of the sixth Earl Cowper by his wife and children. The perpendicular style Brocket Chapel at the east end was added in 1930 by the future first Lord Brocket, who included a medieval-style tomb for his first wife. Opposite the church is Brocket Park's main gateway.

Turn right along the rising road to pass the Mill House. Just beyond the seat (left and before reaching the church) go left to a gateway. Keep forward as the track bears away to the right by a barn. Go over the stile to pass between paddocks. At the end go through the barrier (or over the stile) and keep by the fence on the left. The path briefly meets the river at a bend before continuing ahead and becoming fenced. A kissing gate leads to a short, wide grassed path linking the field with the Great North Road. To the left is a bridge spanning the river.

Cross directly over the road to the trees to find the path continuing down steps. Soon more steps lead up and down to the riverside. Go under the motorway and up a few steps on the far side into Stanborough Park.

(If the riverside path under the bridge is flooded return to the road and turn left. At the far end turn left by The Bull to go under the motorway and enter Stanborough Park.)

STANBOROUGH PARK was opened in 1970: its lakes were dug on former farmland and fed by the upstream Lemsford Springs, and the course of the river was slightly straightened. The 126 acre (51 hectare) recreation area is part of Welwyn Garden City, which lies to the north, and has been slowly developed since garden city pioneer Sir Ebenezer Howard bought the land in 1919 from the Hatfield and Panshanger estates (page 43). Boating takes place on the north lake and sailing on the south. Fishing for carp, roach and bream is popular, but anglers have to compete with the herons. The Stanborough Reed Marsh Reserve by the river at the park's southern end includes one of Hertfordshire's largest reed beds and was once a source for thatching material. In the park the River Lea is inhabited by coots and moorhens, and towards the park's southern end there are water rats living along the bank. The Walk's entry at the north end was built as early as 1978 by the Welwyn and Hatfield Upper Lee Valley Group volunteers.

Bear half-left to walk between the river (left) and the lake (right). At the lake's far end go over the footbridge and under the road to reach the southern lake. The information centre and café are to the left. The Walk continues ahead between the lake (left) and the river (right).

At the lake's southern end only continue with the river to see the reed bed in the nature reserve.

The main Walk leaves the river by bearing left with the lake. Once round the corner and on the grass bear over to the right to go through the gate and under the King's Cross railway line viaduct. Beyond the high bridge a lane runs ahead to Woodhall Farm. Turn left at the junction to reach a road at Mill Green.

MILL GREEN The 18th-century working mill sells flour and is open Tue–Fri, 10am–12.30pm and 2–5pm, and at weekends afternoons only; admission is free (tel. 01707 271362). Stoneground wholemeal farmhouse loaves made with freshly ground Mill Green Flour are on sale at branches of Simmons the Bakers at downstream Hertford and Ware.

At the lodge turn right to join the main road by Leaside House. Cross a braid and the main River Lea and pass the entrance to Bush Hall (right). At the traffic lights cross the road before continuing ahead.

To visit the Mill or the Green Man pub go left before the bridge.

The main Walk continues along the main road, which crosses high above a dual carriageway to reach a junction on the edge of Hatfield (ahead). (The Walk continues left over the grass to the side road at the back of Hatfield Park.)

To reach Hatfield Station: Do not turn left but continue ahead past the turning, keeping the wood to the left. Where the pavement turns away from the road go half-left with the path to join the Old Hatfield Road, which stays with the wood. Go left at another junction into Park Street. Just beyond Park Meadow (right) the pavement is on the right and separated from the road. Go under the Hatfield House viaduct and, before the Horse and Groom, turn right up a passage. A road leads up to the Hatfield Arms by the main road. Hatfield Station is opposite.

Refreshments

Harpenden: Inn on the Green (off main street opposite Station Road); open all day.

Harpenden: Pizza Express, High Street; open all day.

Batford (Harpenden): Marquis of Granby, Marquis Lane; on Walk; open some lunchtimes and every evening.

Wheathampstead: The Bull; open all day.

Lemsford: Long and Short Arm; open all day.

Lemsford: The Sun Inn; open all day.

Stanborough Park: Coffee Shop; open in summer.

Mill Green: The Green Man, Mon–Fri, 12–2.30pm and 5.30–11pm; weekends open all day.

Accommodation

Harpenden: Carlton B&B, 8 Carlton Bank, Station Road, AL5 4SU; tel. 01582 765756.

Harpenden: Hall Barn, 20 Sun Lane AL5 4EU; tel. 01582 769700.

Harpenden: Laurels Guest House, 22 Leyton Road AL5 2HU; tel. 01582 712226.

Harpenden: Milton Hotel, 25 Milton Road AL5 5LA; tel. 01582 762914.

Harpenden: 81 Luton Road AL5 3BA; tel. 01582 460402.

5. Hatfield to Hertford

Hatfield Station (WAGN Railway) to
Hertford East (WAGN Railway)

Maps:	**5–7**
Distance:	**8 miles (13km)**
OS Maps:	**OS Explorer 182 (St Albans and Hatfield) and 174 (Epping Forest and Lee Valley)**

From Hatfield the Walk turns east to follow at first the main road behind Hatfield Park before rejoining the river. Beyond Holwell, near Essendon, the route is along another former railway line now known as the Cole Green Way. The old railway hotel, still to be found by the former Cole Green Station, is now a handy open-all-hours pub and the natural break on this section, which reaches Hertfordshire's county town.

HATFIELD was heathland when King Edgar gave this spot to the monks of Ely about 970. A century later Domesday Book records four mills on the River Lea. In 1497 Bishop Morton of Ely built a palace here and later, as a royal palace, this became home to the young Princess Elizabeth, who was here when she became queen in 1558. Her first Privy Council meeting was held in the Great Hall, when she made William Cecil her secretary of state. His son held the same office under James I, who soon exchanged his own home, Theobalds, 18 miles (29km) downstream, for Hatfield. Since then Hatfield House has been the principal Cecil residence and came back into prominence when Robert Cecil, third Marquess of Salisbury, was Queen Victoria's prime minister. The House and the surviving wing of the royal palace stand in 530 acres (214 hectares) of parkland, with a 42 acres (17 hectares) of Jacobean garden laid out by Charles I's gardener

John Tradescant the Elder. Hatfield House (entrance opposite the station) is open April–Sept, weekends 1–4.30pm and Tues–Thu 12–4pm; admission charged. The Park is open daily 10.30–8pm (Fri 6pm); admission charged.

The church, at the top of Fore Street, is dedicated to Ely's St Etheldreda. Lady Jane Grey's mother was baptised in the font. Charles I attended a service here in 1647 whilst a prisoner at Hatfield House. After the Restoration Samuel Pepys often worshipped here, travelling up from London on the new coach service. Buried

Elaborate stonework at Hatfield House

inside are Robert Cecil, who received James I at Theobalds, and Lord Melbourne (see 'Brocket Hall', Walk 4). Outside the west door is the tomb of John Whitemore, who died in 1801, having lived in three centuries under five monarchs. The oval Marychurch (Roman Catholic and at the bottom of the hill) was completed in 1970. Hatfield House and the Eight Bells both feature in *Oliver Twist* by Dickens, who visited in 1835. When the railway arrived in 1850 the second Lord Salisbury ensured that it ran nearby, and soon the viaduct was built to provide the direct access over the old town for Hatfield House.

The famous Hatfield Aerodrome (home to the 'Mosquito' and 'Comet'), Hatfield University and Hatfield New Town are to the west of the railway.

To reach the Walk from Hatfield Station: Cross the road to walk down the side of the Hatfield Arms to Old Hatfield. At the bottom of the hill turn left into the old main road to go under the viaduct. Follow the pavement, which becomes separated from the road for a short distance. Where they rejoin there is Hatfield Park to the right. Cross the end of Park Meadow (left) and, on approaching a T-junction, keep ahead over the grass to turn right along Old Hatfield Road. At the end join the main road pavement and pass the lodges at an entrance to Hatfield Park. Take the first right to join the Lea Valley Walk.

Face the oncoming traffic on the slip road to join the main Hertford Road. Keep ahead, using the grass verge where possible. Just after crossing the River Lea there is a brief view (right) of an island in The Broadwater formed by the river as it passes through Hatfield Park.

Continue past a lonely bus stop, and just beyond the huge road sign look out for the waymarks where the path takes a double bend, leaving the traffic to run behind the trees and alongside the Hatfield Park fence. Later the path crosses a footbridge over a Lea tributary and briefly rejoins the road.

At the northern entrance to Hatfield Park go through the kissing gate on the left and follow a woodland path gently downhill towards the Cecil Saw Mill. Go through the kissing gate and ahead along the road which bends to cross the Lea. At once go left, with the estate road running parallel to the river.

At the next bend leave the road to continue ahead on a bridleway. For the next 1½ miles (2.4km) there is only an occasional glimpse of the water as the path runs ahead along the side of the shallow valley.

At a path T-junction a wide drove runs to the right, south, uphill for one mile (1.6km) to The Candlestick pub at remote West End hamlet (see below).

Soon after the boundary hedge switches to the left there is a brief view, half-right, of the tower of Essendon Church. At the far end the path passes through a wood and avoids a small pit to emerge on an approach road to Three Valleys Water offices. Turn right to meet a main road at a bend.

Essendon is ½ mile (800m) to the right (see below).

MAP 6

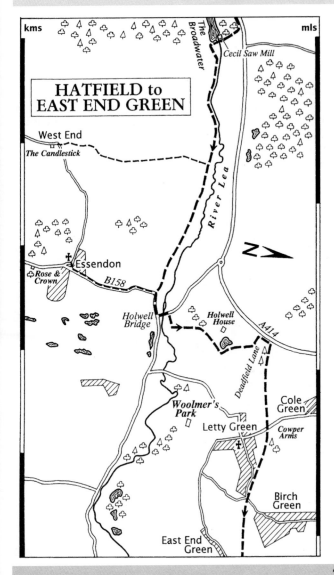

kms

mls

The Broadwater

Cecil Saw Mill

HATFIELD to EAST END GREEN

West End

The Candlestick

River Lea

N

† Essendon

Rose & Crown

B158

Holwell Bridge

Holwell House

A414

Deadfield Lane

Woolmer's Park

Letty Green

Cole Green

Cowper Arms

Birch Green

East End Green

MAP 7

The Walk continues ahead and down to the bus shelter at the Holwell Bridge junction. Turn left into Holwell Lane, walking on the right side. Cross the River Lea and just after a gateway (right) go through the kissing gate (right).

Bear round to the right to follow the edge of the field. At the far corner turn left uphill to follow a sometimes almost invisible boundary. Keep to the left on reaching the dividing undergrowth, and at the top corner continue ahead into the wood. There is a ditch to the right as the path rises through the wood. On arriving at a fence ahead, note the

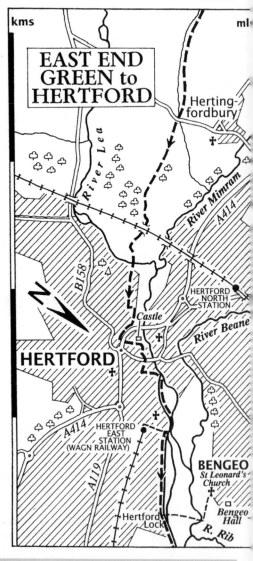

EAST END GREEN to HERTFORD

view of 18th-century Holwell House, then follow the path as it turns right. The way is now between a fence (left) and the wood, passing a seat by a pond (right) to a kissing gate at a bend. At a junction ahead, before the house, turn right and soon there is a view of a lake (left) and a distant tower. The wide way bears round to the left (past a redundant kissing gate) and soon there is an information board and a fenced viewpoint above the lake.

HOLWELL HOUSE LAKE There was extensive gravel extraction here in the 1980s but now the land has been restored by Redland Aggregates. The lake was an irrigation pond during the extraction process. From the south side can be seen (to the south-east) Stratton's Folly at Little Berkhamstead – a 100ft tower (30.5m) erected in 1789 for Admiral John Stratton to watch shipping movements on the Thames.

On reaching a field go through the kissing gate and follow the enclosed path, which joins a bridleway at another kissing gate. Turn left along this path, known as Deadfield Lane, but just before the main road go right along a woodland path. At the far end there is a view over fields to houses at Cole Green. Go down the slope to turn right onto the Cole Green Way, which runs to Hertford.

COLE GREEN WAY, a bridleway route between Welwyn Garden City and Hertford, opened in 1978 along the former Welwyn–Hertford railway line built in 1858 and closed in 1966.

The path is at first in a cutting before running between fields to cross high above a road, where there is a view of the Cowper Arms, to the former Cole Green Station. (The station approach road links to the pub.)

COLE GREEN The Cowper Arms, once the railway hotel, is named after the Cowpers of Panshanger Park, although the present pub sign shows a relative – the poet and hymn writer William Cowper (1731-1800), who wrote *John Gilpin* (see 'Ware', Walk 7). The entrance to Panshanger Park can be seen on the far side of the green to the north, but the mansion, built in 1806 for the fifth Lord Cowper and inherited in 1913 by Lady Desborough, was demolished in 1954. It was one of the first houses in England to have a Christmas tree – one is recorded here as early as in 1829. The park still contains the Great Oak of Panshanger – Britain's oldest oak. South of the Cole Green Way, at the end of Station Road, is Letty Green. As children the Queen and Princess Margaret occasionally attended services at its early Victorian church whilst staying with their grandparents Lord and Lady Strathmore at Woolmer's Park on the bank of the River Lea.

After another ½ mile (800m) the trail runs high over the road at Birch Green. But on approaching the next junction the way divides for riders and walkers before the level rises to meet the road to East End Green (right). Continue ahead on the far side. After about ¾ mile (1.2km) there is a view half-left of the green spire of Hertingfordbury Church and soon the way passes over the road leading to the village. (There are steps on the right leading down to the road.)

HERTINGFORDBURY is on the River Mimram, which joins the Lea just outside Hertford. The 13th-century church was largely rebuilt in the 1850s by Earl Cowper of Panshanger Park (page 43). Inside the church the Cowper Chapel contains magnificent family monuments, including one to Judge Spencer Cowper (flanked by two female figures), who early in life was acquitted of murdering a young woman. Under the tower is an effigy of Lady Calvert, whose husband, Lord Baltimore, and children founded Maryland in 1634 and the city of Baltimore. The pew ends were carved by Joseph Mayer of Oberammergau in 1895. The patron of the church is the Queen in her role as Duke of Lancaster – John of Gaunt, the first Duke of Lancaster, once held the manor. Post-impressionist painter Spencer Gore (who often stayed with his mother at Garth House in the lane opposite the church) is buried in a flat tomb, possibly designed by Eric Gill, on the south side of the churchyard. The funeral in 1914 was attended by fellow artists Jacob Epstein, Stanley Spencer and Paul Nash. The White Horse Inn is 16th century behind its 18th-century frontage. Hertingfordbury Park, between the church and the Cole Green Way but once running south to the Lea, was a royal deer park where both Henry VIII and Elizabeth hunted and hawked. The buildings are now a school and nursing home.

The Walk continues ahead on the Cole Green Way past the Hertingfordbury Station House into a cutting. A bridge over the path carries a former Hertingfordbury Park entrance. Where the way divides keep right on the main path to a junction opposite a wood. Turn left to pass under the high railway viaduct carrying the King's Cross–Stevenage line. Follow the track ahead to go through a gate and past Hertford Football Ground. Follow the hedge (right) to cross the River Lea, which is about to be swollen by the Mimram. The lane runs uphill to a road at a bend.

Turn right along the road for only a few yards to cross over and find steps running up through trees. The path, Wallfield Alley, runs on a ledge between gardens and eventually emerges next to the Black Horse in West Street.

Turn right past the pub to reach the centre of Hertford. Go right with the main road and, once round the bend, cross the road by going down the slope and through the underpass. Beyond the steps on the far side cross Castle Street. The White Horse is to the left.

Keep forward into the castle grounds and through the gateway. Turn right and left to walk in front of the castle. At the river turn sharp right and then left at a junction to go through a gateway and ahead to a second gateway by a road. Cross over to continue up Maidenhead Street (past McDonald's) to the Market Place. Turn left down Bull Plain and cross the river onto an island.

Turn right onto the beginning of the towpath, which passes the Old Barge pub and a long row of cottages. Follow the path across a weir, and at the end bear right over another footbridge to reach Folly Bridge over the main channel at the end of Mill Road.

To reach Hertford East Station: Walk down Mill Road. (Note that trains from Hertford East Station run through the Lea Valley to London's Liverpool Street. Hertford North Station, some distance away in North Road, is served by King's Cross trains.)

Refreshments

Hatfield: Eight Bells, Park Street; 11.30am–3pm and 5.30–11pm; weekends open all day.

Hatfield: Horse and Groom, Park Street; 11am–3pm and 5–11pm.

West End: The Candlestick; 11am–3pm and 6pm–11pm; summer weekends open all day.

Essendon: Rose and Crown, High Road; 11am–3pm and 5.30–11pm.

Cole Green: Cowper Arms; open all day; children welcome.

Hertingfordbury: Prince of Wales (turn left at church); free house; open all day.

Hertford: Black Horse, West Street (where Walk enters town); Mon–Thu 11.30am–3pm and 5–11pm; Fri–Sun open all day; ploughman's, soup and French bread and jacket potatoes.

Hertford: The Old Barge; pub on towpath dating from 1843; Mon–Fri 11.30am–3.30pm and 5.30–11pm; weekends open all day; Sun and Mon night no food.

Hertford: also see Walk 6.

Accommodation

Cole Green: 5 Cole Green Cottages SG14 2NL; tel. 01707 333225.

Birch Green: Grange View, 51 Birch Green SG14 2LR; tel. 01992 586189; smoke free.

East End Green: Orchard Cottage, East End Green SG14 2PD; tel. 01992 583494; look out for a footpath short cut on the right after Birch Green or take the East End Green Road; smoke free.

Hertingfordbury: Prince of Wales; tel. 01992 581149.

Diversion to The Candlestick

Walk up the wide-hedged path which bends occasionally as it climbs the side of the valley. At the top there is a gate leading to the road at West End. Go right and then left at the divide to find The Candlestick on the left.

THE CANDLESTICK The small pub was The Chequers until 1966, when it adopted its long-held nickname derived from a past landlord's habit of using just one candle and leaving customers in the dark when he took the candlestick down into the cellar. The isolated pub welcomes walkers. See 'Refreshments' above for opening times.

Return to the Walk either by the outward route or by walking past the gate and downhill to a ford to climb a hill to Essendon. Turn left beyond the church to rejoin the Walk.

Diversion to Essendon

At the corner turn right to follow the road uphill for just over ½ mile (800m).

ESSENDON The church has a square 15th-century tower, and inside a plaque at the east end recalls a surprise German airship attack on the church and village in 1916. Buried in the churchyard is the Revd Robert Orme, whose tomb has a door – the key was placed on the inside, along with a bottle of wine and a loaf, when he was buried in 1843. As a child Beatrix Potter used to stay at Camfield Place, on a Lea tributary to the south of the village, which she described as 'the place I love best in the world'. It was, until her death, the home of novelist Dame Barbara Cartland.

6. Hertford to Ware

Hertford East Station (WAGN Railway) to
Ware Station (WAGN Railway)

Maps:	**7–8**
Distance:	**2 miles (3.2km)**
OS Map:	**OS Explorer 174 (Epping Forest and Lee Valley)**

Navigation on the Lea begins at Hertford and from here the Walk is on the easy to follow and sometimes metalled towpath. At Hertford Lock there is an opportunity to divert to see a rare Norman church. The Lock affords a magnificent view across floodplain meadows towards Ware. But before reaching this small town the path passes the feed of the man-made New River. Ware is recognisable by its unique waterside gazebos.

HERTFORD, one of the smallest county towns, has a hart fording the Lea on its borough seal. An important event here was the first national Church Synod in 672, when Theodore of Tarsus united the north's Celtic Christians with the south's growing church, and created a network of dioceses – as recorded on a stone outside the castle. The first castle was a wooden fort built by King Alfred's son after the river became the boundary between the Saxons (south) and Danelaw (north). The Normans built the mound and massive stone walls. It was stormed by the French in 1216. Edward VI was staying when he became king on the death of Henry VIII. Later Elizabeth I, who took up residence for a fortnight, granted the town its Saturday market charter, which allows no other within a 7 mile radius. On a café-bar in Fore Street a plaque records that it was the home of John Stone, who founded Hartford, capital of Connecticut. Nearby Shire Hall features in Jane Austen's *Pride and Prejudice*. Naturalist and Darwin contemporary Alfred Russel Wallace lived at Wallace

MAP 8

House in St Andrew Street when a child. Biggles House in Cowbridge was home of Captain W.E. Johns, author of the *Biggles* books, during his teenage years (1900-1912). The churches of St Andrew's, All Saints (open Saturday morning) and the Immaculate Conception and St Joseph's are all Victorian buildings on ancient church sites. The Friends Meeting House in Railway Street, built about 1669, is the country's oldest purpose-built Quaker house and was visited by Quaker founder George Fox and William Penn of Pennsylvania fame. Hertford Museum in Bull Plain, occupying a 17th-century building, tells the story of the town's milling and malting (open Tue–Sat, 10am–5pm). McMullen's, Hertfordshire's oldest independent brewery, known locally as Mac's, was founded here in 1827.

To reach the Walk: At Hertford East Station turn right along Mill Lane and keep forward at a junction to reach the river.

Just before Dicker Mill Bridge go right down onto the towpath with the water to the left. There are light industrial buildings opposite and houseboats before Hertford Lock and The Meads is reached.

HERTFORD LOCK is the highest lock on the Lee Navigation and the first of 18 between Hertfordshire and London. The view from the lock is of the vast water meadow known as The Meads.

From here there is a diversion to St Leonard's Church at Bengeo, Hertfordshire's oldest building (see below).

THE MEADS, never having been ploughed, has a diverse ground flora, with at least 23 plants rare in Hertfordshire. There are also many common wild flowers, and the lady's bedstraw creates a yellow haze. Once the land would have provided a hay harvest before being turned over to grazing from Lammas Day (1 August) until Candlemas (2 February). Winter flooding attracts visiting gulls, waders and ducks – the latter sometimes staying to nest along with lapwings and migrant yellow wagtails. More than 11 species of dragonfly are found here and the chalky hill to the south attracts butterflies. Continuing management by the Hertfordshire and Middlesex Wildlife Trust includes pollarding willows and re-excavating ditches to restore water levels in this rich and rare wetland habitat.

Downstream of the lock the path drops with the water to join the meadow. Soon the river widens, and just before a bend the River Beane can be seen on the far side winding its way to a confluence with the Lea by a lonely house below a cliff. The next lonely building is New Gauge, on the towpath side, marking the point where the Lea feeds the New River.

NEW RIVER is an artificial river dug between 1609 and 1613 to bring pure spring water from Chadwell Spring on King's Mead and the spring at Great Amwell (see Walk 7) into the heart of London. But a link was soon made with the Lea, and in 1856 the present New Gauge was erected over a permanent intake. The idea of a man-made channel was pioneered by Sir Hugh Myddelton, who had made a fortune in the New World and even tried the new fashion of smoking with Sir Walter Raleigh. Strong opposition to the plan from landowners was overcome with support from James I, who was willing to see the course pass close to his new home at Theobalds (see 'Cedars Park', Walk 11). He retained his enthusiasm despite once falling from his horse into the frozen waters of the New River. The original 40 mile (64km)

Plaque at Ware railway station commemorating Robert Stephenson, its designer

circuitous route (to cover 25 miles/ 40km) followed the 100ft contour along the west side of the Lea Valley, allowing the water to reach London by gravity. Although no longer connected to the reservoir at Islington's Myddelton Square, the river does flow as far as Stoke Newington and can be tapped by Thames Water's modern Ring Main. A continuous walking route along the river is being developed.

The path is under some trees as it runs alongside grazed meadow and under the A10 road. Ware Lock is away from the towpath and wedged by the lock islands. (The town can be reached across the bridges or at the next crossing.) The towpath crosses a stream to run under trees. Beyond the end of the large island there is a high crossing leading to Ware Church and the main street.

WARE See Walk 7 for Ware, the gateway to the Lee Valley Regional Park.

Between here and the Town Bridge there are views of Ware's gazebos.

WARE'S GAZEBOS There were once 27 18th-century gazebos on the riverside lining the many pub gardens. Now there are five restored examples as well two recent additions.

Cross a former maltings inlet to reach Town Bridge, flanked by the Saracen's Head and Bridgehouse pubs.

To reach Ware Station: Turn right along Amwell End and go left into Station Road just before the level crossing.

Refreshments

Hertford: Black Horse, West Street (where Walk enters town); Mon–Thu 11.30am–3pm and 5–1pm; Fri–Sun open all day; ploughman's, soup and French bread and jacket potatoes.

Hertford: The Old Barge; on towpath; Mon–Fri 11.30am–3.30pm and 5.30–11pm; weekends open all day; Sun and Mon night no food.

Hertford: The Greenhouse Café, 33 Railway Street; 8.30am–4.30pm (Sat 5pm); closed Sun.

Hertford: McDonald's, Maidenhead Street; open all day.

Accommodation

Hertford: 19 Greenways SG14 2BS; tel. 01992 302538. Smoke free.

Hertford Lock: Bengeo Hall (near ancient church); tel. 01992 505897.

Hertford: Balls Park Campsite, Mangrove Road; Mar–Nov; tel. 01992 586696 before 8pm.

Contact Hertford TIC: Market Place; tel. 01992 584322.

Diversion to Bengeo

Cross the bridge at the downstream end of Hertford Lock, and after a second bridge bear half-right across the grass to find a narrow footbridge spanning the River Beane. Cross the water and at once bear sharply round to the left to follow a path uphill across the field to a kissing gate in a corner. Turn right round the edge of a churchyard to find the entrance to St Leonard's Church.

ST LEONARD'S, Bengeo, is a rare example of a Norman village church complete with a 13th-century wall painting and a hidden hermit's door. Dating from 1156, this is claimed as the oldest building in Hertfordshire. Open weekends 2.30–5pm from late Spring Bank Holiday weekend to September.

7. Ware to St Margarets

*Ware Station (WAGN Railway) to
St Margarets Station (WAGN Railway)*

Maps:	**8–9**
Distance:	**2 miles (3.2km)**
OS Maps:	**OS Explorer 174 (Epping Forest and Lee Valley)**

At Ware's Town Bridge the river enters the Lee Valley Regional
Park. The navigation and its towpath at once slip out of Ware to
turn south along the Lee Navigation. The path is partly sheltered
by trees and there are occasional seats. The optional short
diversion to Amwell leads to one of the prettiest stretches of the
New River, where there is a pub, as well as teas in the church on
summer Sundays. Towards St Margarets, the Lea Valley Walk is
joined by the Meridian Way before crossing the Greenwich
Meridian Line for the first time. There are picnic tables at about
halfway along this section.

WARE comes from the Saxon word for weirs, and as well as
being a stop on the road to Cambridge and the north the town
was also an important port. Henry VII passed through, on his
way to Norfolk's Shrine of Our Lady at Walsingham, as did
James VI of Scotland as he came south in 1603 to claim the
throne as James I of England. One side of the High Street is
lined with inn archways which once led to stables as well as
the riverside gazebos (see 'Ware's Gazebos', Walk 6). Pepys,
Defoe and Isaac Walton all stayed at The George (now
Barclays Bank). Ware is famous for its 10ft square Great Bed
of Ware mentioned in Shakespeare's *Twelfth Night*, Ben
Jonson's *Epicoene* and George Farquar's *The Recruiting Officer*.
The bed, capable of holding twelve people, was displayed in
local inns, including the White Hart (now HSBC), where
Prince Ludwig of Würtenburg slept in it. The Saracen's Head

THE LEA VALLEY WALK

Waterside gazebos at Ware

had it in 1870 before it went on show at Rye House (Walk 9). The bed is now in the Victoria and Albert Museum. Old maltings buildings recall the barley which grew here in the valley. Grain was sent by water to London during its 1665 Great Plague, and Ware was rewarded with the Freedom of the Port of London – as signified on the town's arms. St Mary's Church, with a very tall tower, was part of a Benedictine monastery founded in 1078 and belonging to St Evrou in Normandy. It closed in 1415 (prior to the Battle of Agincourt), and some stones may be incorporated in The Priory opposite. This was a Franciscan Priory, where Catherine of Aragon stayed for a time after her divorce. Priory Lodge is Ware Museum (open Sat 11am–4pm; Sun 2–4pm; free). In 1778 William Godwin, future husband of feminist Mary Wollstonecraft, was the first minister of a new chapel (now Delta Graphics) in Church Street. Tarlings ironmongers in the Hight Street has remarkable ceilings, having possibly been built for Henry VII's mother. It is also claimed as the house where, in William Cowper's poem *John Gilpin*, the runaway horse stopped after a dash up the Lea Valley.

Near Ware Lock can be seen the words *Allen & Hanbury* remaining on a former factory now owned by Glaxo. The filled-in archway is on the line of the Roman Ermine Street.

South of the level crossing and New River is Amwell House (part of a college), home from 1740 to 1783 of Quaker poet John Scott, whose hilltop gazebo and grotto, admired by Dr Johnson, can be visited. (To reach the grotto, which has six cool rooms linked by tunnels, turn right along the main road and left up Scotts Road to find the entrance just beyond The Grotto road. Open Sat and Bank Holidays, Apr–Sep, 2–4.30pm; free but torch required.)

To reach the Walk: From Ware Station turn left to the level crossing and then go right to Town Bridge.

From Town Bridge follow the towpath, with the water on the left. Across the river is The Bridgehouse pub garden. Soon there is a view (right) of the converted Ware Flour Mills, which once produced Frenlite Flour. After ¼ mile (400m) the path and the navigation bear sharply right whilst the Old River Lea continues beyond the weir on the far side. After a footbridge the way ahead is on a straight line running south-east for 1½ miles (2.4km). Over to the left are the hills at the entrance to the Ash Valley beyond the Old River Lea. Halfway along there is Hardmead Lock and a lane. (The best turning for Great Amwell is further on.) Soon after, the path passes under the Amwell Walkway Bridge.

AMWELL WALKWAY BRIDGE opened in 1991, replacing a bridge erected in 1863 to carry the railway branch line to Buntingford. The line was closed in 1964 and has been replaced by a footpath route from Amwell to the Old River Lea and on to the valley of the River Ash, which joins the Lea. The new bridge now also carries the 260 mile Meridian Way, which joins the Lea Valley Walk at St Margarets to the south.

Beyond the picnic tables the path rises at a bridge carrying the path from the Amwell Quarry Nature Reserve viewpoint on the far bank (left).

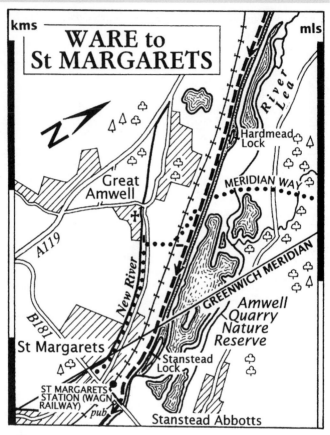

MAP 9

AMWELL QUARRY NATURE RESERVE is a former gravel pit which, since 1983, has become a flooded lake surrounded by woodland. In winter this is one of the best places in the country to see the smew – at least 20 of the ducks have been spotted here. More than 100 other species can be seen over the year.

The path to the right of the bridge leads to the attractive village of Great Amwell (see below).

A quarter of a mile further on, just as the navigation widens, the Greenwich Meridian Line passes unseen across the water and towpath (between a seat and trees ahead). Beyond Stanstead Lock (which has a rare swing bridge between the gates) there is a former maltings (rebuilt as housing, right) as the Old River Lea rejoins from the far side. The combined river turns a corner to reach the bridge linking Stanstead Abbotts (far bank) with St Margarets.

To reach St Margarets Station: Go up the slope onto the road and turn right.

Refreshments
Ware: Ocean Fish Bar, Amwell End (road leading to level crossing); Mon–Sat 12–2pm and 5–10pm.

Ware: Kelly Ann Tea Room, West Street; 9am–4.30pm, Sun 10am–4pm.

Ware: Down to Earth vegetarian café, 7 Amwell End (road linking bridge to station); Mon–Sat 8am–5.30pm.

Great Amwell: George IV pub behind church; 11am–3pm and 6–11pm.

Great Amwell: Teas at church; May–Sep, Sun 3–5pm.

Accommodation
Ware: 145 Cozens Road, SG12 7JB; tel. 01920 464204.

Contact Hertford TIC: tel. 01992 584322.

Diversion to Great Amwell
At the Amwell Quarry Nature Reserve bridge follow the path, right, which is joined by the Amwell Walkway and Meridian Way. Cross the railway level crossing to reach a road. Take the steps almost opposite up to the New River and turn right.

Barge on the river at Ware

GREAT AMWELL comes from *Emmewelle*, meaning *Emma's Well*, which is now a dry hollow with a stone inscribed with words probably by John Scott (see above). Opposite are islands in the New River, and on the second is a memorial to Sir Hugh Myddelton (see 'New River', Walk 6) who 'conveyed this stream to London' bringing 'health, pleasure and convenience to the Metropolis of Great Britain'. (There is an Amwell Street at end of the river in Islington.) In the churchyard the Mylne tomb has a plaque to Robert, who designed Blackfriars Bridge and, as New River engineer, added the island monuments. (He is buried in St Paul's Cathedral.) He lived here at Amwell Grove by the river, whilst his son's home was Flint House (up the hill but not visible or open), where there is a column from the first Blackfriars Bridge. Inside the partly Norman church (open summer, Sun 3–5) is a pulpit from Addington Palace. The huge royal arms were for a time exhibited at Rye House (Walk 9).

8. St Margarets (Stanstead Abbotts) to Rye House

St Margarets Station (WAGN Railway) to
Rye House Station (WAGN Railway)

Maps:	**9–10**
Distance:	**1¼ miles (2km)**
OS Map:	**OS Explorer 174 (Epping Forest and Lee Valley)**

Here the Lea Valley Walk is also the Meridian Way, which joins from the New River west of St Margarets Station. St Margarets and Stanstead Abbotts face each other here across the narrow river at the start of this short towpath section, where the new riverside homes opposite soon give way to countryside as the path bends under a high by-pass. The reward at Rye House is a 400-year-old pub with an unusual frontage and the historic Rye House Gatehouse alongside a nature reserve.

ST MARGARETS is on the western bank of the river, where the church dates from Norman times (open Sat 10.30am–12.30pm; turn right from the station and left into Hoddesdon Road to pass The Crown). The full name was the Chapel of the Blessed Virgin Mary at St Margaret's Thele (meaning St Margaret's Island). Draining has reduced the river to its present channel, but the parish, the smallest in Hertfordshire, is still island shaped. For 115 years from 1316 this was a collegiate church with five priests, and on the outside north side there are traces of the larger building. A glass screen at the back has illustrations, engraved with a dentist's drill, of local scenes including a Meridian marker. Buried by the altar is Colonel Henry Lawrence, president of the Council of State under Cromwell, who, having opposed the execution of Charles I, survived the Restoration to continue living at the

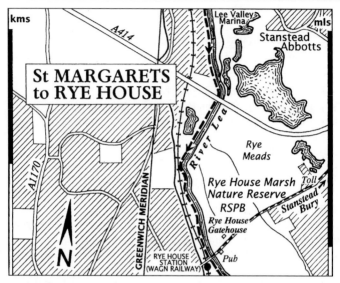

MAP 10

next door manor house. A memorial on the north sanctuary wall to the Pratt family mentions Frances Cecilia Cowper as being a relative of the poet William (see 'Cole Green', Walk 5). Opposite the church today are typical Lea Valley glasshouses – once trays of tomatoes were sent weekly from this area to London's Spitalfields Market.

STANSTEAD ABBOTTS *Stanstead* is derived from an Anglo-Saxon word meaning *stony place* and *Abbotts* is a reference to the *Abbot* of Waltham (Walk 12), whose abbey later owned the village. In the High Street there is the impressive 1752 Stanstead Hall, which was probably the miller's house. Later a Dr Hunt, who lived there with his two spinster sisters, is said to have used the brick tower as an escape route to visit a female friend at Batchelors Hall opposite. The mill stream crosses the far end of the High Street to pass through the maltings. Also by the stream is the Red Lion, dating from

1538. Clock House School opposite was provided by the Baeske family, who are commemorated in the redundant church of St James to the south-east of the village (page 67). The Victorians built the present church, situated just beyond the horses and ducks warning signs in Cappell Lane.

To reach the Walk from St Margarets Station: Turn left out of the station entrance to reach the bridge linking St Margarets and Stanstead Abbotts with the Lea Valley Walk below.

Keep the water to the left as the towpath runs past the sculpture at the Riverside Green by the Jolly Fisherman and the Lee Valley Marina opposite. After ½ mile (800m) the Stanstead Abbotts mill stream, flowing off the Old River Lea, can be seen entering on the far side.

The river makes a slow double bend where the Stanstead Abbotts by-pass runs high overhead. As the path straightens out the river is parallel with the Rye House Marsh Nature Reserve (far bank), which runs as far as the bridge.

To reach Rye House Station: Go up the slope on to the road and turn right.

Refreshments:

St Margarets: Taxi Office, St Margaret's Station; 6.30am–midnight.

St Margarets: Jolly Fisherman pub by river; basic hours and all day Fri–Sun.

Stanstead Abbotts: Bridge Shop, High Street; open to at least 6pm.

Stanstead Abbotts: Lord Louis pub in High Street.

Stanstead Abbotts: Red Lion; historic pub at far end of High Street; open all day.

Accommodation

Contact Hertford TIC: tel. 01992 584322.

9. Rye House to Broxbourne

Rye House Station (WAGN Railway) to
Broxbourne Station (WAGN Railway)

Maps:	**10–11**
Distance:	**3 miles (4.8km)**
OS Map:	**OS Explorer 174 (Epping Forest and Lee Valley)**

This is a beautiful stretch, which includes the junction with the Stort Navigation and the attractive Dobbs Weir, where the Lee Navigation again leaves the Old River Lea. There are riverside pubs at Rye House, Dobbs Weir and Broxbourne. The towpath, for the first time without its metalled surface, again crosses the Meridian.

RYE HOUSE includes the remains of a moated manor house, a unique pub, a nature reserve, the Showmen's Guild winter quarters, a station and a new village. *Rye* means *atter eye* or *at the island*, and is a reminder that Rye House, built in 1443, stood on an island among the flood meadows. The road is a former causeway and remains a toll road with a gate at the far east end.

The house was the centre of the 1683 Rye House Plot to kill both Charles II and his brother, the future James II, as they rode along the lane from Newmarket to London. Rye House was owned by Richard Rumbold, who had been a guard at Charles I's execution, and he planned to overturn a cart in the lane and attack the trapped royal party. However, the conspirators were thwarted by the king, who returned home a week early. When the plot was revealed executions followed, and Rumbold fled to Holland. The Duke of Monmouth was temporarily saved from the gallows only to die for his unsuccessful Monmouth Rebellion against James II two years later, when Rumbold was also executed for taking part

Rye House, centre of the Rye House plot to kill Charles II

in the simultaneous Argyle Rebellion in Scotland.

In 1857 Henry Teale, landlord of the pub, turned Rye House into an attraction for Londoners and City firms, who staged dinners in a 120ft long barn with 'cathedral glass windows'. The house furnishings included the Great Bed of Ware (see 'Ware', Walk 7). Today the surviving gatehouse is owned and managed by the Lee Valley Regional Park Authority, and has been restored as a magnificent example of early English brickwork. It is open (Good Fri–Sept, Sun, Bank Holidays and school holidays; admission charge; tel. 01992 702200) for visitors to view an exhibition and a model of the original house, and to climb up onto the roof to enjoy the view and take a look at the barley sugar chimney. Children should look on the ground floor for the 'secret panels' to see the Rye House conspirators' secret meeting-place.

THE RYE HOUSE PUB, once the King's Arms, dates from about 1600. Its magnificent windows are of the same date, although were added only about 1870, having been brought from a house in Cheshunt. The garden had a maze – an added attraction. Henry Teale died in 1876, and the present name was adopted in 1904 when the family sold up. The pub was virtually rebuilt in 1980. There was no station here when the railway opened in 1843 so the pub was allowed to sell tickets to fishing club members, and trains were halted by using a red flag. In 1849 a small booking office opened to test the market, and new pub landlord Teale sent his family daily to St Margarets by train to boost ticket sales. Eventually the

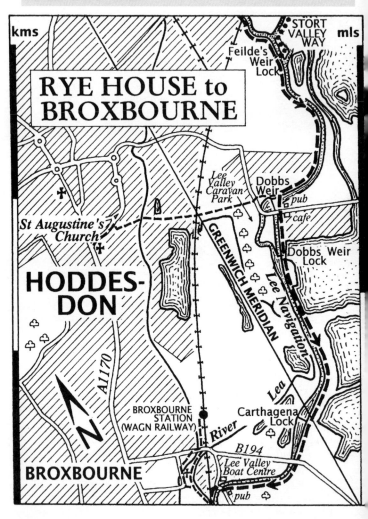

kms   mls

STORT VALLEY WAY

Feilde's Weir Lock

RYE HOUSE to BROXBOURNE

Lee Valley Caravan Park

Dobbs Weir

pub

cafe

St Augustine's Church

Dobbs Weir Lock

HODDES-DON

GREENWICH MERIDIAN

Lee Navigation

A1170

Lea

BROXBOURNE STATION (WAGN RAILWAY)

Carthagena Lock

River

B194

BROXBOURNE

Lee Valley Boat Centre

pub

MAP 11

Brocket Hall was designed for the Lamb family and completed in 1780

Hatfield House was once home to Queen Elizabeth I

The New River near Hertford

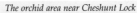

The emperor dragonfly

The orchid area near Cheshunt Lock

The bittern

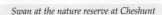

Swan at the nature reserve at Cheshunt

The river section known as the Edmonton Cut runs past Pickett's Lock (and the leisure centre)

The Lea Bridge, the third on this site, opened in 1892

Rye House: the remains of the moated manor at the centre of the 1683 Rye House Plot

Dobbs Weir, where the River Lea and navigation divide

The river at Broxbourne

Great Eastern Railway (WAGN Railway's predecessor) ran Bank Holiday excursions to here from north London and Bishop's Stortford.

RYE HOUSE MARSH NATURE RESERVE, to the north of the house, embraces part of riverside Old Rye Mead and Thames Water's sewage treatment works. There are wide paths and five hides which give the opportunity to see kingfishers, kestrels, ducks and woodpeckers all year round. This RSPB reserve is primarily for environmental education, but individuals are welcome (open 10am–5pm or dusk, if earlier; admission charge; tel. 01279 793720).

THE SHOWMAN'S GUILD GROUND, where fun fairs go in winter, is on the site of a permanent fairground where, within living memory, donkeys could be hired at the gate on a Sunday for a ride up the then rough causeway.

The toll road passing the pub runs east for just over a mile to Stanstead Abbotts Church (see below).

To reach the Walk from Rye House Station: Turn right at the main road to find the towpath at the bridge. The towpath is reached on the upstream side of the bridge. Walking south the water should be to the left. Across the river there is soon a go-cart track and by the path a view of Sainsbury's Rye Park distribution centre. The railway bridge ahead carries the Cambridge–Liverpool Street line. Round the bend is the Feilde's Weir and Lock with the River Stort joining from the far side above the weir.

FEILDE'S WEIR The Stort Navigation runs north for 14 miles (22.5km) into Essex from this junction on the Hertfordshire border to Bishop's Stortford. The meandering River Stort was made navigible between 1766 and 1769 by building 15 locks and numerous artificial cuts. The towpath between nearby Roydon and Sawbridgeworth is part of the Stort Valley Walk route. Members of the Feilde family are commemorated in Stanstead Abbotts Church (see below).

Riverside pub at Dobbs Weir

Past the power station (right) the river takes a long double bend down towards Dobbs Weir. On the way the towpath passes over an inlet. There is a weirpool and picnic area just before the Fish and Eels pub at Dobbs Weir.

DOBBS WEIR has existed under this name since at least 1604. Here the river and navigation divide. The Fish and Eels was one of the inns favoured by Isaak Walton.

At the weir continue ahead only for Hoddesdon (1½ miles, 2.4km) (see below).

The Lea Valley Walk continues over the footbridge above the weir to reach a road. Cross over to find the towpath, for the first time, to be on the opposite bank. Walking south the water should be to the right. The path is wide as it runs past first Dobbs Weir Lock and across the Greenwich Meridian Line just yards before Carthagena Lock, which is noted for its hanging flower containers above the gates. Beyond the Broxbourne–Nazeing road bridge the river bears round to the east to give a view of Broxbourne Church tower up on high ground. At the sharp bend by The Crown cross the bridge to the Broxbourne bank. Go left, with the water to the left, to cross the Mill Stream bridge.

To reach Broxbourne Church: Go right to follow the millstream and continue ahead up Mill Lane. At the top of the hill, and before the New River, go right to the church (see 'Broxbourne', Walk 10). To reach the station continue ahead over the bridge and bear right to follow path to The Kingfisher and station entrance.

To reach Broxbourne Station: Go right to follow the millstream to the Old Mill. Cross the millstream and turn left through the Old Mill to follow the stream (left). At a high footbridge, before the railway bridge, go left over the water. At a junction keep ahead under the road bridge to find the station beyond the car park.

Refreshments
Rye House: Historic Rye House pub open all day; children's menu; cups of tea and coffee; fenced riverside garden with children's play equipment.

Dobbs Weir: Fish and Eels; open all day.

Carthagena Lock: Tea, drinks and ice cream in summer.

Accommodation
Dobbs Weir: Lee Valley Caravan Park; campsite; Mar–Oct; tel. 01992 462090.

Contact Hertford TIC: tel. 01992 584322.

Diversion to Stanstead Abbotts Church
From Rye House follow the toll road over the river and between Rye House pub (right) and gatehouse (left). The road crosses the Tollhouse Stream before running in a straight line to the automatic tollgate. Continue forward and soon the road climbs to a T-junction. Cross over to find steps opposite leading into the churchyard.

STANSTEAD ABBOTTS CHURCH, dedicated to St James the Great, is a mile from the riverside village (see 'Stanstead Abbotts', Walk 8). It is thought that the village was here on high ground until a bridge over the river was built at the end of the High Street, and the village gradually moved down to the road by the river crossing. But remaining here with the church is Stanstead Bury, a former rest-house for monks travelling between Waltham Abbey (Walk 12) and Ely. The church's 15th-century tower is by Westminster Abbey master mason William Stowell, who added the south-east chapel at Broxbourne (page 72). The brick north chapel was added in 1577 and was almost certainly seen by Elizabeth I, who stayed at Stanstead Bury the next year. Earlier in her reign she had stopped here on her way to Theobalds (see 'Cedars Park', Walk 11) and again before arriving at Hertford Castle (page 48). Her hosts, commemorated in the chapel, were Edward Baeshe, general surveyor for the victuals for the Royal Navy through four reigns from Henry VIII, and his wife, Jane (daughter of Ralph Sadleir of Homerton; page 102). Also commemorated is the Feilde family, who gave their name to Feilde's Weir (see above). Opposite the entrance is a tablet to Henry Teale (see 'Rye House', above), who was married here. The St James window next to the pulpit is a memorial to his daughter. There are also memorials to the Booth family of gin fame, who lived nearby. The church retains its box pews and three-decker pulpit. Services are held only on special occasions such as St James's Day (nearest Sunday afternoon to 25 July). The church is open Sundays, Jun–Sep, 2.30–5pm.

Diversion to Hoddesdon

Do not cross Dobbs Weir but continue ahead with the Old River Lea. The path leads to a road. Cross over and continue ahead on a very wide path, which later narrows. Cross the railway line, keep ahead to a kissing gate and go along the side of a field, where the path rises to a gate by the New River. Go left to cross the footbridge, and keep ahead along a sunken path to emerge outside a school. Follow the road past Riversmead (left) to a junction opposite the Co-op. Turn left up Charlton Way and at St Augustine's Church cross over into the High Street. Hoddesdon town centre is to the right.

HODDESDON may be derived from a Dane called *Hogge*, who lived at, or on, the site of Hogges Hall (64 High Street). Surprisingly, the church dates from only 1732, but the market square clocktower is on the site of a 1336 chapel built for pilgrims travelling from London to Walsingham in Norfolk. More than a thousand horses would be stabled here overnight, and there are still ancient pubs which were built to cater for the London–Cambridge traffic, such as the 16th-century White Swan and Salisbury Arms on the west side. The Bell Inn on the east side may be named after the bell which rang (as the curfew and Shrove Tuesday pancake bell) from the pilgrim chapel opposite. The nearby house with the grapes decoration, on the corner of Brewery Road, replaced the Thatched House Inn where Isaak Walton stayed. An early edition of his *Compleat Angler* was printed in Hoddesdon on a press now in Washington's Smithsonian Institute. The Toc H shop opposite is at least 17th century and has a chapel upstairs. Almost next to the church in Amwell Street is Myddelton House, where the son of Sir Hugh Myddelton (of New River fame) lived. Once on the high pavement opposite the church was the house where in 1829 Harriet Auber, inspired but missing a pen, scratched on the window the words of the hymn *Our blest Redeemer ere He breathed*. Lloyds TSB (68 High Street) was home of road engineer John McAdam (see 'Broxbourne', Walk 10) from 1827 until his death in 1836. The Grange, on the corner of the High Street and Cock Lane, was once a school, where pupils included the future prime minister A.J. Balfour. Further south is Lowewood Museum (open Thu–Sat, 10am–4pm), which displays local inn signs and glass from Theobalds (see 'Cedars Park', Walk 11). Market days are Wednesday and Friday.

To reach Broxbourne Station from Hoddesdon: Either catch a bus in the High Street or return to the New River and turn right to walk with the water on the right. Steps lead down to the station.

10. Broxbourne to Cheshunt – River Lee Country Park

*Broxbourne (WAGN Railway) to
Cheshunt Station (WAGN Railway)*

Maps:	**11–12**
Distance:	**3 miles (4.8km)**
OS Map:	**OS Explorer 174 (Epping Forest and Lee Valley)**

The river winds south out of Broxbourne between Silvermead grazing meadows and Nazeing Marsh. At King's Weir the water divides into the Old River Lea and the navigation, with its towpath running in an almost straight line to Cheshunt through two locks. Trees completely screen new development to the west, and to the east can be seen Hayes Hill on the Essex side of the Lee Valley Park. There are picnic tables just before Cheshunt Lock and a spectacular orchid area at its best in early June.

To reach the Walk: On leaving the station follow the pavement ahead but just before the main road cross the station road to go down steps. Turn right through the car park to pass under the road bridge. Keep ahead to go over the millstream. Turn right to follow the water (right) to the Old Mill. Cross the water to continue on the far side past a café and under the railway to the towpath.

Scenic route to Walk via church: On leaving the station go through the kissing gate (right) and climb the steps to the New River. Turn left to follow the water to Nazeing New Road by The Kingfisher. (To see the Pulham kiln go down the side of Beech Court next to The Kingfisher.) Cross the road and turn right. After a few yards bear left on a path across the green to reach a road. Turn left over the New River bridge to pass the church. Go left down Mill Lane to reach the river beyond the railway bridge.

MAP 12

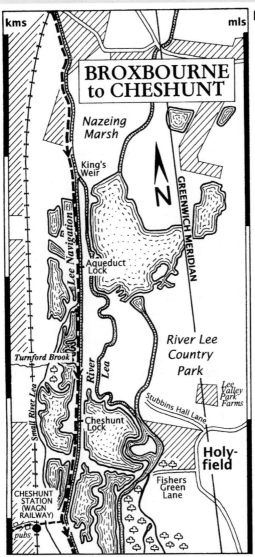

kms — mls

BROXBOURNE to CHESHUNT

Nazeing Marsh

King's Weir

Lee Navigation

Aqueduct Lock

GREENWICH MERIDIAN

N

River Lee Country Park

Lee Valley Park Farms

Turnford Brook

River Lea

Stubbins Hall Lane

Small River Lea

Cheshunt Lock

Holy-field

CHESHUNT STATION (WAGN RAILWAY)

Fishers Green Lane

pubs

BROXBOURNE means *badger stream*. The church, dating from 1450, was built on high ground above the River Lea 150 years before the New River (see page 50) began to flow on two sides, giving a moated appearance. Inside on the south side (to left of door by font) is a memorial to John McAdam, 'the great improver of the British roads', who invented tar macadam and is said to have feared the success of the railway which arrived here four years after his death in 1836. Further along, above the next door, is a memorial to Edward Christian, whose brother led the mutiny on the 'Bounty'. The Norman font, of course, comes from elsewhere. Below the church is the ruined Old Mill, which is mentioned in the Domesday Book. The avenue of trees leads across the green to the Anne of Cleves pub by the main road. On the opposite corner is the Mustard Pot (a former hotel). Beyond the pub are the 1728 Monson almshouses opposite The Bull, which is on the site of a 1521 inn. The kiln by The Kingfisher dates from 1845 and was used for producing terracotta garden pots.

From the millstream the water is to the left. After ½ mile (800m) the houses on the far bank give way to Nazeing Marsh, and after a further ½ mile there is King's Weir. Beyond here the path widens into a track running to Aqueduct Lock. There are occasional glimpses of Turnford Marsh Lakes (right).

AQUEDUCT LOCK takes its name from the aqueduct above the gates spanning a millstream, known as the Small River Lea, from the Old River Lea to work a now lost mill at Cheshunt.

Soon after a turning to Turnford Brook, there is Fishers Green Bridge leading to Holyfield Marsh.

HOLYFIELD MARSH is named after a convent which stood nearby. The path crosses the marsh to follow the Old River Lea to Fishers Green, below the hilltop Holyfield, where Hayes Hill and Holyfield Hall Farms are sited – working farms open to visitors, and still within the Lee Valley Regional Park.

Just beyond Cheshunt Lock there is another crossing, leading to Fishers Green, and then Redpoll Hide (right). Soon there is a signposted path to Cheshunt, but this leads only to the High Street and not to the station or the church. Continue to the bend ahead, where Cheshunt and Cheshunt Station can be easily reached.

To reach Cheshunt Station: Go down the slope and over the stile to walk through a car park and over the Small River Lea (where a youth hostel will soon be built) to a level crossing.

The church at Broxbourne

Refreshments

Broxbourne: Café in Mill Lane.

Accommodation

Broxbourne: Church View, 80 Station Road, EN10 7AN; tel. 01992 460807.

Broxbourne: Higher Drift, Allard Way, EN10 7ER; tel. 01992 463301; off Bell Lane, north of roundabout.

Cheshunt: 14 Ashdown Crescent EN8 ORE; tel. 01992 628853; turn off the towpath at the first Cheshunt signpost after Redpoll Hide; go right into Elm Drive.

11. Cheshunt to Waltham Abbey

Cheshunt Station (WAGN Railway) to Waltham Cross Station
(WAGN Railway)

Map:	13
Distance:	1¼ miles (2km)
OS Map:	OS Explorer 174 (Epping Forest and Lee Valley)

This short stretch, with two locks, runs to the main road by Waltham Abbey, which can be seen across Waltham Marsh on the far bank.

CHESHUNT comes from *Chestrehunt*, in Domesday Book, meaning *Roman fort in a wood*. The old village is in Churchgate, a mile to the west (see below). Windmill Lane, linking the station to the main road, recalls the windmill which stood north of the lane and opposite The Windmill pub until 1845.

To reach the Walk: Turn right out of the station to follow Windmill Lane over the Small River Lea and through the car park.

Turn right. The view ahead is of the Highbridge footbridge. Just beyond Waltham Common Lock there is a glimpse of Friday Lake on the far side. After Powdermill Cut joins (left; see page 80), there is the wide expanse of Waltham Marsh and a view (half-left) of Waltham Abbey's tower well before the bridge.

At the bridge there is a path to the right leading to Theobalds Grove (see 'Diversion', below).

The main Walk continues on the towpath as the canal turns and there is a view of the main Waltham Cross–Waltham Abbey main road immediately below Waltham Town Lock.

To reach Waltham Abbey (Walk 12): Turn left and cross the Old River Lea.

To reach Waltham Cross Station: Continue under the bridge and up the slope by the Old English Gentleman. Turn left and

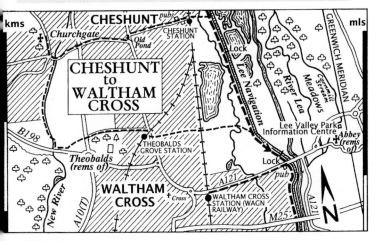

MAP 13

follow the main road to the station entrance on the railway bridge.

Refreshments
Cedars Park: Tearoom; Tue–Sun 10am–dusk; daily in August.

Accommodation
Cheshunt: 14 Ashdown Crescent EN8 ORE; tel. 01992 628853; turn off the towpath at the first Cheshunt signpost after Redpoll Hide; go right into Elm Drive.
Cheshunt: Churchgate Lodge, 197 Churchgate Road; tel. 01992 637462.

Diversion to Cheshunt
Turn left out of the station forecourt to walk along Windmill Lane, passing The Windmill pub. At the Old Pond roundabout go left and right into College Road. Cross the A10 by the footbridge and continue ahead past The Crocodile pub and over the New River. Turn right into Churchgate.

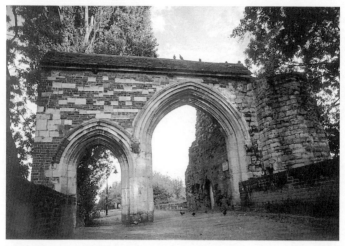

The gatehouse at Waltham Abbey (see also Walk 12)

CHESHUNT'S CHURCHGATE The Roman road Ermine Street runs along the west side of the old village. The church was built in the 15th century but has Victorian additions. The patron of the church remains the Marquess of Salisbury, since the nearby manor house, Theobalds (see 'Cedars Park', below), once belonged to the Cecil family. The prominent royal arms inside the church are Charles II's. The Old Parsonage (by the Victorian postbox) was built in 1500, and there Tumbledown Dick, Oliver Cromwell's son Richard, died in 1712 after living incognito in the village. The Green Dragon, dating from the 16th century, was originally used as overnight accommodation for ambassadors visiting James I at Theobalds. The village is dominated by the buildings of the former Bishop's College, now council offices, but once a training college for the Countess of Huntingdon's Connexion sect and, from 1909 to 1968, an Anglican theological college. The tall tower was added in 1870. Bishops Court, on the corner of Churchgate and College Road, replaced Grove

Cottage, the inspiration for *The Small House at Allington* by Anthony Trollope, who lived at Waltham Cross.

To reach a station from Cheshunt's Churchgate: Either catch a 363 bus to Waltham Cross or walk to Theobalds Grove via Cedars Park. Return to the New River and turn south with the water to the left. Cross the first bridge, but before the road go left along the side of the field to join Theobalds Lane. Cross the A10 dual carriageway to continue ahead. Cedars Park is on the right (see below). At the far end turn right for Theobalds Grove Station.

Diversion to Theobalds and Theobalds Grove Station

A few yards past Highbridge footbridge turn sharp right up the slope and ahead on the path signed 'Theobalds Grove'. The hard red surface crosses the Small River Lea. Keep ahead at a divide to go over the level crossing and up Trinity Lane. At the main road go right past Christ Church and Theobalds Grove Station, and left into Theobalds Lane to find Cedars Park on the left.

CEDARS PARK, now a public park, is the site of the few remains of Theobalds. The mansion was built in the 1560s for Robert Cecil, chief minister to Elizabeth I, who visited 15 times. Cecil became Lord Burghley and was succeeded by his son Sir Robert Cecil, who in 1603 welcomed James VI of Scotland on his way south to claim the English throne as James I. He stayed for four days and took such a liking to the building and gardens that within four years he had persuaded Cecil to exchange it for the royal estate at Hatfield (Walk 5). The stone loggia at Hatfield is a copy of the one on the original house here, which was demolished under Oliver Cromwell. James, who introduced elephants and camels as well as building a 9 mile wall around the estate, died here in the presence of his son Charles, who also set out from here to enter London as King. A century later Isaac Watts, who wrote 600 hymns including *O God, our help in ages past*, lived in a house on the site. By 1763 a new mansion called Theobalds Park had been built to the west beyond the New River.

12. Waltham Abbey to Enfield Lock

Waltham Cross Station (WAGN Railway) to
Enfield Lock Station (WAGN Railway)

Maps:	**13–14**
Distance:	**1½ miles (2.4km)**
OS Map:	**OS Explorer 174 (Epping Forest and Lee Valley)**

The river here was first improved for navigation in the late 12th century by the Abbot of Waltham. The abbey church was once part of England's most important monastery and is described by Simon Jenkins, author of *England's Thousand Best Churches*, as a four-star church and one of England's top hundred. The Norman church still divides the market town on the Greenwich Meridian Line from the rich watermeadows. In the former abbey grounds is the Lee Valley Park Information Centre. From here the Walk is a short easy section to Enfield Lock, where a large artificial island created for an arms factory has recently become a waterbound residential community.

To reach the Walk: At Waltham Cross Station turn right to go up steps to the main road. Turn right and follow the road as far as the Old English Gentleman pub, which is before Waltham Abbey.

WALTHAM ABBEY church was the heart of an Augustinian monastery founded in 1177 as part of Henry II's penance for St Thomas Becket's murder. *Waltham* means *weald homestead*, and the first church was built here in about 1030 to house a miraculous cross brought by King Canute's standard bearer. King Harold is said to have prayed before the cross in 1066 on his way to defeat at the Battle of Hastings, and afterwards he was supposedly buried in the church – the now truncated building has left a tombstone outside the church's east end dedicated to his memory. Queen Eleanor's body rested here in the abbey church on its way from Nottinghamshire to Westminster Abbey – hence the nearby cross on the main road at Waltham Cross, which is the last in the chain of 12 before Charing Cross. Later the monastery was a refuge for Richard II during the Peasants' Revolt. It is suggested that the Church's cataclysmic break with Rome had its seeds here in 1529 when future Archbishop Thomas Cranmer, who was temporarily resident, discussed Henry VIII's desire for a divorce during a royal visit. The large abbey was the very last to be closed by Henry VIII and so survived until 1540. Among those displaced by closure was the organist and composer Thomas Tallis, who eventually found a post at Greenwich (page 118). The landmark tower was built shortly afterwards in Mary I's reign to replace a central one which collapsed. Most of the buildings have gone, but the impressive Norman nave remains, with an east end window by Burne Jones, and a rare display of the signs of the zodiac painted on the ceiling in 1860. The Lady Chapel has a fascinating 15th-century doom painting, and in the crypt below (visitor centre) is a Virgin statue hidden at the Reformation and only recently found. The effigies of Elizabethan Sir Edward Denny and his wife (right of high altar) have been described as having the appearance of relaxing in front of a television. In the 19th century Waltham's bells inspired Tennyson's poem *Ring Out Wild Bells.* Here too the carol *Hark, the herald angels sing* was first set to the now familiar Mendelssohn tune. Lychgate House, the teashop in the churchyard, dates from 1420 – the date 1600 above the door refers to improvements – and was probably a priest's house. The abbey church is usually open 10am (Sun 12 noon)–4pm (or BST 6pm); free.

Cornmill Meadows, reached by a subway to the north of the abbey, is a dragonfly sanctuary best visited in summer. Here, in an area bounded by the Old River Lea and the Cornmill Stream (dug in the 12th century), can be found (between May and September) at least 21 different types of dragonfly – half the native species – making this the best place to see dragonflies in Greater London

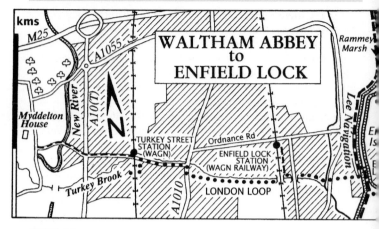

MAP 14

and the Home Counties. Alongside (east side of stream) is the former GLC arboretum, bisected by the Greenwich Meridian Line, which can be followed between two granite sculptures.

On the west bank of the Old River Lea, and reached by way of Powdermill Lane off the roundabout, is **Waltham Abbey Royal Gunpowder Mills**. The abbey mills were taken over for gunpowder production as early as 1561. The government took control in 1787 following difficulties in the American War of Independence. Gunpowder was taken down the Lea in sailing barges to the Thames and on to Woolwich for the Napoleonic Wars. In 1815 William Congreve, comptroller of the Royal Laboratory at Woolwich, whose son worked at Bromley-by-Bow (see Walk 18), introduced a number of improvements. By the Second World War, when the Dambuster bombs were being made, the workforce totalled 3,000. The Ministry of Defence withdrew in 1991, leaving an overgrown area which included 30 herons' nests and one of the UK's largest flocks of siskins. Rampant alder and willow, planted for making charcoal (a gunpowder ingredient), are a major feature. The factory buildings and internal canals will be opening to the public shortly.

In the town the Epping Forest Museum (Fri–Tue 2–5pm; free; tel. 01992 716882), housed in two Tudor buildings, is at the east end of Sun Street just before the Crooked Mile junction. Crossing Sun Street, and marked on the ground, is the Greenwich Meridian Line. Market day is Tuesday and Saturday. The Tourist Information Centre is located in Highbridge Street, close to the entrance of the abbey church.

The Lee Valley Park Information Centre is north of the abbey church (open daily in summer 9.30am–5pm; Nov–Easter Tue–Sun 10am–4pm; tel. 01992 702200).

Go down the slope onto the towpath at the side of the Old English Gentleman. After a few yards there is the Riverside Café and a high bridge over Hazlemere Marina. Here the river bends to pass a pumping station and run alongside an industrial estate. On the far bank there is a long 'island' belonging to Islington Sea Scouts with a flood channel running behind on the east side.

Beyond the M25 bridge the path is alongside the now raised Rammey Marsh. Ahead is Rammey Marsh Lock.

RAMMEY MARSH LOCK dates from 1863, when the straight cut was dug. However the lock has an 1835 bridge.

The path now runs in a straight line, with some houseboats opposite, as far as a missing bridge at the bend where the water divides.

Here there is a link with the flood channel which creates Enfield Island. Soon, across the water, there is a row of cottages (dating from 1857) on a thin strip of land with water on both sides and the main island behind. Ahead is the bridge leading to Enfield Island.

ENFIELD ISLAND VILLAGE is the new name for the former Royal Small Arms Factory site, which is surrounded by water. The factory's first buildings on the artificial island were ready for use in 1816, using a mill for power. New buildings were added in the 1850s as the private gun trade failed to satisfy government standards. At one time as many as 1,700 people worked on the island, where the famous Lee-Enfield rifle was manufactured – *Lee* comes not from the river

The clock tower of the old Enfield Rifle factory

but *James Paris Lee*, who developed the weapon. The Government Row cottages facing the towpath near the lock originally housed some of the workers. The island once had a church, a school and a police station. The factory, which closed in 1987, preceded most buildings in Enfield Lock, and even Enfield Lock Station was at first called Ordnance Factory Station. The residential development has preserved some buildings, including the clock tower.

For a direct route to Enfield Lock Station go right to pass The Greyhound and keep ahead over the road junction and down Ordnance Road.

After The Greyhound (right) the towpath is parallel to a road. Across the water can be seen the cottages on Enfield Island. At Enfield Lock the Lea Valley Walk is briefly joined by the London LOOP.

LONDON LOOP is the 150 mile (241km) London Outer Orbital Path which circles the capital using 24 sections co-ordinated by the London Walking Forum. For more information send an s.a.e. to London Walking Forum, Corporation of London, PO Box 270, Guildhall, London EC2P 2EJ.

Here the LOOP can be followed west for 1½ miles (2.4km) to Myddelton House (see below), which is famous for its garden, created by the world renowned plantsman E.A. Bowles, and is the head office of the Lee Valley Regional Park Authority.

To reach Enfield Lock Station: Turn right at Enfield Lock to follow the London LOOP route along a footpath and over a footbridge spanning a main road. Behind there is a view of the Sewardstone Hills in Essex and the reservoir. Continue forward alongside the Turkey Brook and over Newbury Avenue. At the end go right along Bradley Road to the Railway Inn on the corner at Ordnance Road. Enfield Lock Station is to the left by the level crossing.

Refreshments
Waltham Abbey: Philpott's Tea Rooms, Lychgate House at Abbey; 9am–4pm or later.
Waltham Abbey: Welsh Harp, Sun Street; dates from 1520.
Waltham Abbey Riverside: Old English Gentleman pub (at river bridge).
Waltham Abbey Riverside: Riverside Café (on towpath south of bridge); open all day.
Enfield Lock Island Bridge: The Greyhound, alongside new island bridge; 11am–3pm and 6.30–11pm.
Turkey Street: The Sun and Woolpack; open all day.
Turkey Street: The Turkey.

Accommodation
Waltham Abbey: 74 Highbridge Street EN9; tel. 01992 768115.
Waltham Abbey: 22 Elm Close EN9 1SQ; tel. 01992 764892.

Tourist Information
Waltham Abbey: 4 Highbridge Street EN9 1DE; tel. 01992 652295.

Diversion to Myddelton House

Myddelton House is served by Turkey Street Station, which is closed on Sundays.

Turn right at Enfield Lock to follow the London LOOP route along a footpath and over a footbridge spanning a main road. Behind there is a view of the Sewardstone Hills in Essex and the reservoir. Continue forward alongside the Turkey Brook and over Newbury Avenue. At the far end by Bradley Road (right) go left over Turkey Brook to follow the opposite bank and cross the railway at the footbridge. Continue north along Prince of Wales footpath beside the Turkey Brook (right) in Albany Park. At the far end the path is enclosed before meeting a road. Go right into St Stephen's Road to reach a main road. Go right and left into Turkey Street just before The Sun and Woolpack. When the LOOP turns left off Turkey Street keep ahead past Turkey Street Station. Use the pedestrian underpass to cross the dual carriageway and continue forward over the New River to a junction. Myddelton House is ahead.

MYDDELTON HOUSE is a detached section of the Lee Valley Park and its headquarters. The house, named after Sir Hugh Myddelton of New River fame (see page 50), dates from 1815 and replaces one occupied since 1724 by the family with the controlling interest in the New River Company. Henry Carington Bowles, who died here in 1918, was the River's last governor. His son, the famous gardener E.A. Bowles, was born in 1865 and lived here continuously until his death in 1954, when the house was still without electricity or a telephone – Bowles feared that calls would distract him from gardening. The garden, which embraces part of a filled-in loop of the New River, contains the market cross from nearby Enfield and Bowles' 'Lunatic Asylum' area, where a contorted hazel is known as 'Harry Lauder's Walking Stick'. The garden is open Mon–Fri 10am–4pm, and (Easter–October) Sundays and Bank Holidays, 2–5pm; admission charge.

13. Enfield Lock to Ponders End

Enfield Lock Station (WAGN Railway) to Ponders End Station (WAGN Railway)

Maps:	**14–15**
Distance:	**2 miles (3.2km)**
OS Map:	**OS Explorer 174 (Epping Forest and Lee Valley)**

Here the towpath is on the eastern bank running alongside the vast 420 acre (170 hectare) King George's Reservoir, opened in 1913 and the largest in Greater London. Half-way along a new bridge provides a route to Brimsdown Station where trains stop at least hourly. Ponders End station does not have a Sunday service.

To reach the Walk: At Enfield Lock Station turn right and right again into Bradley Road. Just before a bridge go left and follow the Turkey Brook. Continue ahead over Newbury Avenue, and at a junction bear right to cross the main road by a bridge. The path ahead leads directly to Enfield Lock.

ENFIELD LOCK: see 'Enfield Island Village', Walk 12.

At Enfield Lock cross the road bridge below the lock to find the towpath on the opposite bank near Rifles pub. Follow the path for a short distance to cross the entrance to the Swan and Pike Pool, where there is a LOOP information board.

Leaving the LOOP, continue ahead along the towpath to pass under a former railway bridge which carried the line from the arms factory. Shortly afterwards there is a view across to the mouth of the Turkey Brook, which rises near Potters Bar to flow across Enfield Chase and enter the Lea just swollen by the Small River Lea. Ahead, as the river bends, is a large power station.

Over to the left is the massive King George's Reservoir, whilst

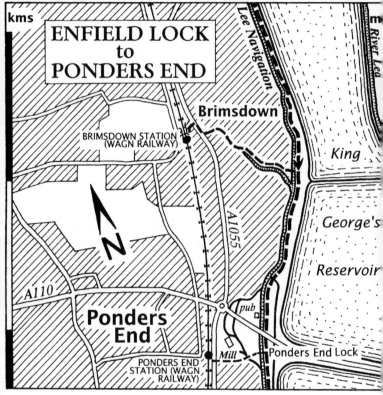

MAP 15

alongside the path there may be horses or cattle. Early on there is a glimpse of the capital ahead in the form of Canary Wharf's pointed roof. The western bank is Brimsdown Factory Estate.

BRIMSDOWN FACTORY ESTATE The large distribution centre for breweries is on the site of the Ruberoid factory, which produced roofing materials for most of the 20th century from 1910. Mossops Creek on its south side originated in the 19th century as an inlet for loading barges from a gravel pit. Further south is the overhanging canopy of the former British Waterways transhipment depot. Just downstream on the same bank is the end of Ponders End's Duck Lees Lane (see 'Ponders End', Walk 14).

The blue footbridge just above Mossops Creek gives access to the path alongside the creek and nearby Brimsdown Station (see below).

Four tall tower blocks behind the mill are today's landmarks at Ponders End on the far bank. The millstream can be seen on the right just before the towpath draws level with the Navigation Inn. Pass under the flyover to reach Ponders End Lock and the bridge.

To reach Ponders End Station: Cross the bridge to follow Wharf Road to Mill Lodge at the far end. Use the high footbridge to cross the main road and reach the station.

Refreshments
Enfield Lock: The Greyhound

Accommodation
Enfield: tel. 020 8378 3784 for bed and breakfast availability.

Diversion along Mossops Creek
Cross the blue bridge. Where the path divides go left to follow the creek. At the far end go through a gate and turn right along Stockingswater Lane past Macro (right) to reach the main road (Mollison Avenue). Turn right and cross the dual carriageway at the traffic lights to go down Green Street to Brimsdown Station. McDonald's is to the right and the Isaac Walton pub is on the far side of the level crossing.

14. Ponders End to Tottenham Hale

Ponders End Station (WAGN Railway) to Tottenham Hale
(WAGN Railway and London Underground)

Maps:	**15–16**
Distance:	**4 miles (6.4km)**
OS Map:	**OS Explorer 174 (Epping Forest and Lee Valley)**

Ponders End, still with a working mill, was the cradle for several great 19th-century inventions. This section, known as the Edmonton Cut, runs past Pickett's Lock (famous for its nearby leisure centre which at first took the lock's name) and past Tottenham Marshes. On the way there are tempting diversions to both the Lee Valley Leisure Centre and Bruce Castle which could easily fill a day.

PONDERS END The Ponder family lived at this end of the Enfield parish in the 14th century. The mill, mentioned in Domesday Book, is now Wright's Flour Mill, run by the sixth generation producing flour and bread mixes. In 1867 George Wright moved into the early Georgian East Mill House to work with the Ponders End miller at the weatherboarded watermill dating from 1789. Wheat would arrive by barge, but the water-powered milling gave way to electricity in 1909. This remote area attracted small factories, and inventor Sir Joseph Swan came to Duck Lees Lane in 1886 to work on his light bulb invention before joining forces with America's electrical pioneer to form Ediswan. Around the same period Swan's colleague Sir James Dewar invented the Thermos flask and had its prototype made here before manufacture began further south in Tottenham. Ediswan invited Ambrose Fleming to join the company, and his thermionic valve began the technological revolution enjoyed in the 20th century. The Binatone building, opposite the Granville Tavern, is the

Flour mill at Ponders End. There has been a flour mill here since medieval times

remaining Ediswan building. The Navigation Inn is the former Metropolitan Water Board pumping station built in 1899.

To reach the Walk from Ponders End Station: Cross the parallel main road using the high footbridge to reach Mill Lodge. Continue ahead along Wharf Road to find the towpath on the far side of the bridge.

The water is to the right. The view to the left is of the William Girling Reservoir and soon on the far bank there is the Lee Valley Leisure Centre golf course. The former NatWest Tower in the City of London can be seen ahead shortly before the bend to Pickett's Lock.

PICKETT'S LOCK This is the start of the Pymmes Brook Trail. The nearby Lee Valley Leisure Centre, opened in 1973 as the Pickett's Lock Centre, is one of the largest in the country. This is to be the site of the new National Athletics

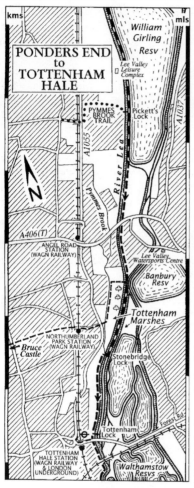

MAP 16

PONDERS END to TOTTENHAM HALE

Stadium, which will host the World Athletics Championships in 2005 (open weekdays 7am–10.30pm and weekends 8am–9.30pm).

PYMMES BROOK TRAIL follows the Pymmes Brook for 10 miles (16km) up to a lake on Monken Hadley Common near Cockfosters. Although the trail ends here the brook enters the Lea downstream at Tottenham Hale (Walk 15). A leaflet which includes a map is available from Lee Valley Park Information Centre (tel. 01992 702200).

To reach the Lee Valley Leisure Centre cross the bridge, turning right along Pickett's Lock Lane and right again at the first junction.

At the far end of the reservoir (left) there is a signed path to Chingford (but not the village). Across the water is the tall chimney and looming building of a refuse incineration plant. Pass under a bridge to see TS 'Plymouth', belonging to the

Islington Sea Cadets, on the opposite bank before walking under a series of new road bridges known as the Lee Valley Viaduct. The river emerges in the Lee Valley Trading Estate, with similar large sheds on both banks.

The riverside road is the towpath as far as Chalk Bridge. Cross Chalk Bridge only for the diversion to Northumberland Park Station and Bruce Castle (see below).

Here, where the BT Tower can be seen, the river runs through the remains of Tottenham Marshes. Lockwood Reservoir is to the right before Stonebridge Lock is reached.

At Stonebridge Lock cross the river to continue south with the river to the left. Here, where the towpath was widened in the 1920s to be a leisure promenade, there is water on both sides, for behind the undergrowth to the right is Pymmes Brook. Across the river is a long line of houseboats with gardens. Ahead is Tottenham Lock.

To reach Tottenham Hale Station: Go up the slope to the main road and turn right. Cross Mill Mead Road and continue uphill to cross the railway. Follow the pavement round to the right to find the station served by both underground and mainline trains as well as buses.

Refreshments

Ponders End: Navigation Inn (Beefeater), off Wharf Road.

Ponders End: Horse and Dray, Alma Road (near station).

Lee Valley Leisure Centre: Deep Pan Pizza Co.; 11am to late; also cafés.

Stonebridge Lock: Water's Edge Pub and Café.

Bruce Castle: Café (in castle kitchen); Wed, Thu, Fri and Sun, 2–5pm.

Bruce Castle: Antwerp Arms, Church Road (behind Bruce Castle); open all day.

Accommodation

Ponders End: tel. 020 8378 3784 for bed and breakfast availability.

Lee Valley Leisure Centre: Camp Site; tel. 020 8345 6666.

Diversion to Northumberland Park
Station and Bruce Castle

Cross Chalk Bridge to Tottenham Marshes.

TOTTENHAM MARSHES Once the meadow had channels and reed beds, but it was long used for grazing and growing a hay crop. Among the wild flowers and grasses found here are some from Asia and North America which, as seeds, may have blown off barges. Here, opposite the towpath, it is possible to follow the river as far as the Water's Edge pub at Stonebridge Lock.

From the bridge keep on the path ahead and at the corner bear left onto a grass path. After almost ½ mile (800m) go right over Pymmes Brook to a gateway leading to Watermead Way main road. Cross over to follow Marigold Road opposite. At Marsh Lane continue forward to reach the level crossing and Northumberland Park Station

For Bruce Castle still continue ahead over the main road and up Park Lane. On the left is the easily missed modern St Paul's Church (right) and the dominant Tottenham Hotspur football ground (right). Cross the High Road into Church Road, which passes under the railway bridge. Before the Antwerp Arms (right) go left into New Road to enter Bruce Castle Park. Follow the middle path to Bruce Castle.

BRUCE CASTLE The name recalls Robert the Bruce, who owned the manor for a brief period at the end of the 13th century. Later, when the castle was a refuge from the London plague, Henry VIII met his sister Margaret, Queen of Scots here. Elizabeth I visited in 1568. The present building dates from 1514 but the brick tower alongside, which may have been a falconry, is thought to date from the 1350s. Rowland Hill ran a school here from 1827 to 1833 before going on to invent the Penny Post. The castle is now occupied by Haringey Local History Museum (open Wed–Sun afternoons; free), and collections include post boxes and paintings of the River Lea by John Bonny (1875–1948). The bowling green is laid out in the kitchen garden, which retains part of its 17th-century wall. John Constable painted the nearby church whilst staying in Tottenham in 1806. In nearby White Hart Lane (north) Samuel South and Sons were major suppliers of clay flower pots for the Lee Valley market gardeners from the late Victorian period until 1960.

To reach Bruce Grove Station: Walk down Bruce Grove opposite the castle passing the almshouses (left). The station is on the right at the High Road junction beyond the railway bridge.

15. Tottenham Hale to Lea Bridge

Tottenham Hale Station (WAGN Railway and London Underground) to Clapton (WAGN Railway)

Maps:	**16–17**
Distance:	**2 miles (3.2km)**
OS Map:	**OS Explorer 174 (Epping Forest and Lee Valley)**

The early view is of the townscape on the side of Stamford Hill before the towpath switches sides to run along the edge of Walthamstow Marsh, where Britain's first air flight took place over land which still yields a hay crop.

TOTTENHAM HALE, from the Saxon *Toteham,* means *the home of Totta. Hale* means *a corner of land.* Ferry Lane, leading to the river, recalls the ferry which preceded the bridge. Isaak Walton fished here whilst staying at a pub called The Swan.

To reach the Walk from Tottenham Hale Station: From the main entrance turn left and left again into Ferry Lane to reach a bridge. Turn left down onto the towpath.

Walk under the bridge with the water to the left and at once go over the entrance to the Pymmes Brook (see 'Pymmes Brook Trail', Walk 14). Across the water there are flats on an island. Just before the Gospel Oak–Barking line railway bridge ahead there is the Narrow Boat pub.

Beyond the bridge the Old River Lea joins on the far side. Ahead can be seen the tall spire of Clapton Common's Church of the Good Shepherd (see 'Spring Hill', below). The next bridge carries the main WAGN trains up the Lea Valley. To the right is a beam engine museum reached by the park gate where there is a signpost (right).

MARKFIELD BEAM ENGINE AND MUSEUM Sewage was pumped at this pumping station into the London

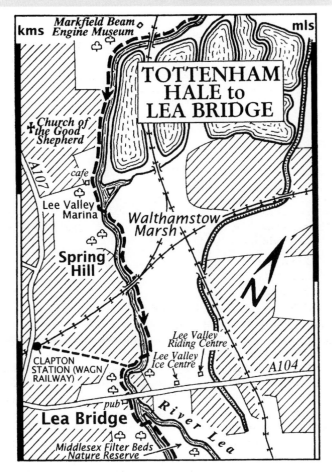

MAP 17

sewage system from 1886 until 1964. The beam steam engine, built at Sowerby Bridge in Yorkshire, was brought here by barge (museum open Mar–Dec 2nd Sunday in month, 10am–3pm; tel. 01763 287331). The filtering beds which once discharged water into the river remain outside. The high grass mounds were created in the late 1960s with earth from the Victoria Line tunnelling.

Ahead, as the river bends by the park, there is a view of Canary Wharf. The far bank, hiding the last of a chain of reservoirs, is lined with houseboats. Two gantries overhanging the path are a reminder that there were many working wharves here. Since 1988 one has been the residential Watermint Quay, at the point where the path leaves Haringey and enters the Borough of Hackney. Across the water is Waltham Forest. Soon there are Tyrell's Yard boathouses and a café at the Spring Hill footbridge – also known as High Bridge.

SPRING HILL The sloping Springfield Park was created in 1905 out of the gardens of three early 19th-century houses, and one survives at the top of the hill as a café. The bottom of Spring Hill had a dock running inland on the south side until the end of the 19th century. The high hill here is evidence of the ice age, when sand and gravel topped by brickearth were deposited on the London clay. In addition to the familiar ducks and geese more than 50 different bird species can be found here. It remains a centre of water activity, with boathouses by the towpath and Springfield Marina opposite. Downstream Horseshoe Bridge recalls the sharp treble bend in the river here until the end of the 19th century. Horseshoe Point is now an island, with Coppermill Stream joining from the east. On the top of the hill is Clapton Common, which at its north end has the landmark Church of the Good Shepherd, built for the Agapemone sect in 1892.

The towpath continues under the bridge. As the Lee Valley Marina opposite ends, so the path crosses the river on Horseshoe Bridge onto Walthamstow Marsh.

WALTHAMSTOW MARSH Parts are cut as near Lammas Day (1 August) as possible, in keeping with the age-old cycle of six summer months of growth followed by six winter months of grazing. The first British flight took place here

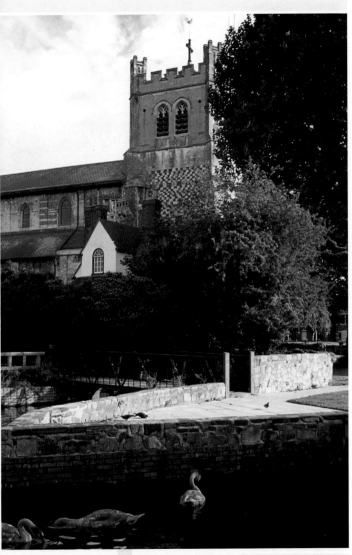

The Norman church at Waltham was once part of England's most important monastery

Waltham Abbey Mills, abandoned in 1991, began gunpowder production as early as 1561

The Lee-Enfield rifle was made at the Royal Small Arms Factory (now Enfield Island Village)

Bromley-by-Bow's remarkable Three Mills has become the place to take the air and relax

The Millennium Dome, seen from Docklands

The 'Cutty Sark' has been in dry dock at Greenwich since 1954

Plaque marking the arches under which the aviator A.V. Roe worked

(see 'A.V. Roe Arches', below), but even the aviator was once ordered off the marsh for 'trespassing on grazing rights'. A ferry, Morris's or High Hill, ran across to the Anchor and Hope, downstream from Horseshoe Bridge, until the 1960s.

Those who wish to remain faithful to the original towpath can walk by the water but there is a broad path, known as Sandy Lane, a few feet back from the riverside. Two now unreachable pubs, including the Anchor and Hope, are across the water at the former High Hill Ferry point. Ahead is the railway bridge used by WAGN trains serving the Lea Valley and Hertford. The railway arches to the left were used by A.V. Roe.

A.V. ROE ARCHES In 1909 aviator A.V. Roe rented two of the brick arches under the railway prior to making the first all-British flight here on Walthamstow Marsh – the engine had been made at nearby Tottenham. At first Roe aimed to fly about as high as the telegraph wires, and one day a would-be suicide begged to be allowed to have a go. In the summer he flew a distance of just 100 feet and soon managed 900 feet. (To see the commemorative plaque go under the bridge and left over a footbridge to follow a boarded walk for a short distance. The plaque can be seen to the left across a fenced wildlife refuge.)

Continue along the towpath. Soon, over to the left, can be seen the spire of St Saviour's in Walthamstow flanked by two tower blocks. The main path rises to run alongside a playing field. Before reaching the looming Lee Valley Ice Centre ahead cross the river at the footbridge. On the far side there is the unmarked back entrance to the King's Head pub on Middlesex Wharf.

MIDDLESEX WHARF The King's Head once had a dock running inland on its upstream side. Downstream on the opposite bank there is still an indication of the once sharp bend here which, when straightened, briefly left an island. The timber yard and downstream path by North Mill Fields face the former Essex Wharf, which is a reminder that the river was the county boundary.

Continue with the water now to the left alongside Middlesex Wharf timber yard as the river bends to North Mill Fields at Lea Bridge.

To reach Clapton Station: At North Mill Fields at once turn right alongside the timber yard to follow Southwold Road up to the Crooked Billet pub on the main road at Clapton. Turn left for Clapton Station.

Refreshments

Tottenham Hale: The Narrow Boat pub, on towpath downstream of bridge; open all day.

Spring Hill: Riverside Café; open all day.

Lea Bridge (approach): The King's Head, Middlesex Wharf (by footbridge from Marshes).

Clapton: Crooked Billet pub, Clapton Road (by station); open all day.

Clapton: Nice Plaice fish and chip shop, corner of Southwold Road (by station); 12–9.30pm except Sun.

16. Lea Bridge to Hackney Wick

*Clapton Station (WAGN Railway) to Hackney Wick Station
(Silverlink Metro)*

Maps:	**17–18**
Distance:	**2 miles (3.2km)**
OS Maps:	**OS Explorer 174 (Epping Forest and Lee Valley) and 162 (Greenwich and Gravesend)**

The Walk still has a rural open feel thanks to Hackney Marsh. It is only after Marshgate Bridge, leading to the western Homerton bank, that the route begins to feel urban and enclosed for the first time since Luton. Here there are the workshops and stores for such institutions as the Royal Opera House and a famous television studio.

To reach the Walk from Clapton Station: Turn right out of Clapton Station and go right down Southwold Road. At the river turn right for Lea Bridge and walk under the bridge.

LEA BRIDGE There has been a bridge here since 1745, when there was also a toll gate. The Mill Fields recall the mill which stood at the junction of the Old River Lea and the Hackney Cut. The Princess of Wales pub, the most southerly waterside pub, dates from the 1860s, but was named the *Prince of Wales* until the death of Diana, Princess of Wales, in 1997. The Ship in Distress, behind, once had water on the inland side as part of Lea Bridge Dock. The stone building in between was a school as the lane's name, School Nook, indicates. Nearby Clapton to the west at the end of Lea Bridge Road was a hamlet on the pilgrim route from London to Waltham Abbey and Walsingham. In 1654 John Evelyn went to see a local garden (Community College site by Brooke Road), which he described as 'one of the neatest and most celebrated in England'.

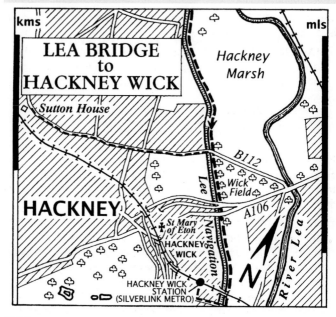

kms

mls

**LEA BRIDGE
to
HACKNEY WICK**

*Hackney
Marsh*

Sutton House

B112

Lee

HACKNEY

*Wick
Field*

A106

*St Mary
of Eton*

**HACKNEY
WICK**

Navigation

River Lea

HACKNEY WICK
STATION
(SILVERLINK METRO)

N

MAP 18

From North Mill Fields go under the main road bridge to pass the front of the Princess of Wales pub. Across the water is a weir leading to the Old River Lea. The towpath follows the Hackney Cut and, after crossing the entrance to the filled-in Lea Bridge Dock, switches banks at the Pond Lane Bridge (which included floodgates until 1987) to run alongside the wall of the Middlesex Filter Beds.

MIDDLESEX FILTER BEDS were built in 1852 to supply clean water to London. Having become redundant in 1969 the walled area is now a nature reserve, managed by Lee Valley Regional Park Authority, with at least fourteen different species of butterfly.

Beyond the filter beds, as Canary Wharf makes another

appearance ahead, the path is opposite the site of the now demol-ished Hackney Power Station and alongside Hackney Marsh.

HACKNEY MARSH Cattle grazed here in winter under the Lammas land scheme, which allowed for a hay crop to be cut in August, until 1893, when the marshes were purchased from the lord of the manor and declared common land. The bridge at Millfield Road, formerly Marsh Lane, is still known as Cow Bridge. Just below Cow Bridge, until 1855, was a lock known as Brick or Homerton Lock.

Pass under Cow Bridge – first of two footbridges here. The view across the water is of Clapton Park houses on the site of saw mills. At the far end, alongside Marshgate Bridge at Homerton, is the former Matchbox toy factory.

MARSHGATE BRIDGE The words 'Matchbox Toys' can still be seen on the side of the Lesney building by the river. Metal for the famous model vehicles arrived by barge. Lesney is derived from the founders Leslie Smith and Rodney Smith, whose metal model vehicles are the company's best-known products. This west bank is in *Homerton*, which is derived from *Hunburgh's* Farm, owned in the 14th century by the Knights of St John of Jerusalem, who had a mill by the river. The road west rises up Marsh Hill into Homerton High Street, where there is a rare Edward VIII post box. In 1760 Berger's Paints was founded in Shepherd's Lane near the now lost Hackney Brook, which ran to the south of the High Street, feeding both a brewery here and watercress beds before joining the River Lea near Old Ford. At the far west end of the High Street is Sutton House.

To visit Sutton House, a mile away, cross the bridge and walk up the hill to the far end of Homerton High Street (see below).

Beyond the bridge is Wick Field, which is now cut through by two huge road bridges spanning the water. New riverside housing of Hackney Wick, replacing wood yards, lies across the water. Beyond Hackney Wick's two bridges (rail and road) is the canal junction with the Hertford Union Canal.

To reach Hackney Wick Station: Turn sharp right before the gate to go up onto the Carpenters Road bridge. Turn left over the water and go downhill to the Lea Tavern. Keep ahead along Rothbury Road and go right at the crossroads into Hepscott Road, past the stoneyard, over White Post Lane and under the bridge at the far end. The station entrance is on the right. (This is the North London Richmond–North Woolwich line. Stay on the first platform for trains to nearby Stratford.)

Refreshments

Lea Bridge: The Princess of Wales; open all day.

Homerton: Sutton House café bar, High Street; Wed–Sun 11.30am–5pm; closed Christmas holidays.

Diversion to Sutton House

Cross Marshgate Bridge to follow Homerton Road, which becomes Marsh Hill as it climbs out of the river valley. Still continue ahead as the road becomes Homerton High Street. Sutton House is on the left as the road bears right at the far end.

SUTTON HOUSE, the East End's oldest house, was built in 1535 of fashionable brick (and called Bryck Place) for diplomat Sir Ralph Sadleir, secretary to Thomas Cromwell and a judge at Mary Queen of Scots' trial. Later Sadleir's daughter entertained Elizabeth I at Stanstead Abbotts (page 67). The National Trust owned house is named after Sir Thomas Sutton, 'esteemed the richest commoner in England' and founder of Charterhouse school, who died in 1611 and lived next door on the site of Sutton Place. The Wenlock Barn, built 1904, is named after the last Lord Wenlock, Rector of Hackney and a descendant of Lord Wenlock, who lived at another early brick house, Someries (page 27), near Luton. (Open Sun and Wed 11.30am–5.30pm; Sat 2–5.30pm; admission charge; closed Dec–Jan; see 'Refreshments' above.)

17. HACKNEY WICK to BROMLEY-BY-BOW

Hackney Wick Station (Silverlink Metro) to Bromley-by-Bow Station (London Underground District Line)

Maps:	**18–19**
Distance:	**1½ miles (2.4km)**
OS Map:	**OS Explorer 162 (Greenwich and Gravesend)**

In 1664 Samuel Pepys wrote: 'With my wife only to take ayre, it being very warm and pleasant, to Bowe and Old Ford...'. The smells have changed and once beautiful Bow suffers from too much traffic. However, the Mexican tea plant, which gives off an aroma when crushed, can be found by the towpath just below the Greenway – the seeds probably blew off a barge coming up-river with a cargo from a ship on the Thames – and this section's climax is Bromley-by-Bow's remarkable Three Mills, which has become the new place to take the air and relax.

HACKNEY WICK means *outlying farm of Hackney*, but has now become detached from Hackney itself, being surrounded by water on two sides and a motorway on the other two. St Mary of Eton Church in Eastway (which can be seen from the station footbridge) was built in the 1880s, to a G.F. Bodley design, by Eton College for its mission to the East End poor. The impressive entrance is through the tower into a courtyard from Eastway.

To reach the Walk from Hackney Wick Station: Turn left out of the station to go under the bridge. At once bear left into Hepscott Road. Cross White Post Lane to the second crossroads. Turn left along Rothbury Road, which becomes Carpenters Road at the Lea Tavern. On the far end of the bridge go right down to the towpath.

The Lea Valley Walk continues ahead with the Hertford Union branch to the right.

HERTFORD UNION CANAL opened in 1830 as a 1½ mile link between the Lee Navigation and the Regent's Canal, which runs through London to the Grand Union Canal. The arm is sometimes known as Duckett's Cut after Sir George Duckett, who also owned the Stort Navigation (see 'Feilde's Weir', Walk 9).

Among the warehouses by the towpath is the Royal Opera House store. Ahead is Old Ford Lock.

OLD FORD LOCK is just above the point where the Roman London–Colchester road forded the Lea. In the 12th century the Empress Matilda is said to have nearly drowned when crossing here, and her mother, Queen Maud (Henry I's wife), had Bow Bridge built. This area, no longer on a main road, became a centre for the dyeing industry. The four former lock cottages have been converted into the Channel 4 Big Breakfast television studios and the garden often features in the early morning live broadcasts. The Old River Lea, which the Lee Navigation left at Lea Bridge, joins from behind the television studio.

Cross the Old River Lea and bear right to keep the water on the right. The river winds under the Northern Outfall Sewer – now also called The Greenway.

THE GREENWAY is a landscaped path and cycleway which runs along the top of a sewer from Bow to Becton, 4½ miles to the east. It crosses Pudding Mill, City Mill and Waterworks Rivers – all braids of the Lea. There is a fine view of Abbey Mills pumping station. The signage is made from old sewage pipes.

A few yards downstream is the now unseen line of the original Old Ford. The view is of dilapidated back yards of Iceland and Bundock's Wharves. Between two railway bridges – the second carries the DLR and Fenchurch Street–Southend line – is a view of the former Bryant and May factory.

BRYANT AND MAY opened its match factory in 1861 in a former crinoline and candle factory. Timber for the

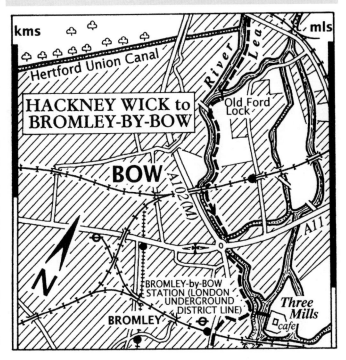

MAP 19

production process was brought up the river. However, there was a high injury rate, and even early deaths, among the mainly female workforce working with high toxic phosphors. Some workers were reported to have glowed in the dark. In 1888, 700 women successfully went on strike for better conditions. The Match Girls Strike was a landmark, and encouraged Will Thorne at nearby Beckton gasworks to enrol new trade union members, who won similar public support and better conditions. The present building, erected in 1911, produced matches until 1979, when it was converted for residential use.

After a short distance the path crosses the Bow Back River entrance and runs up to the roundabout under the Bow flyover below Bow.

BOW is on the west bank and takes its name from the first bridge here, which was built of stone and bow shaped. It had been erected in the early 12th century at the instigation of Queen Maud (see 'Old Ford Lock', above) and soon a port village grew up on the London side to receive goods from Hertfordshire. The church, in the middle of the road, dates from 1311, and today the 15th-century tower has a Victorian addition. In 1940 the funeral of deputy Labour leader and local MP George Lansbury was held here. Fairfield Road, on the north side and named after an annual fair, leads to the former Bryant and May match factory, now called Bow Quarter. Outside the church is a statue, paid for by Theodore Bryant's workers, of Gladstone – it has long been claimed that he is pointing the way to the (now closed) public lavatories below. Bow porcelain was first made on the east bank in nearby Stratford. The present Bow flyover, alleged resting place of Kray victim Jack 'The Hat' McVitie, was designed by Russian Andrei Tchernavin, who escaped the gulag via Finland in 1932.

Cross the dual carriageway ahead with extreme care. Go ahead down the main road, signposted to Tesco. After a few yards go left down Global Approach to a wharf. Soon the towpath narrows and gently winds down towards Three Mills, where the path rises to the Three Mill Lane bridge.

THREE MILLS There was a mill here in Saxon times and at one stage four mills existed. The number is now two. The House Mill was built in 1776 on the site of a pre-Domesday mill. This, Britain's largest tide mill, was driven by river water which had been trapped upstream at high tide. Milling ceased in 1940. The Clock Mill was built in 1817, replacing a weatherboarded mill, but the clock tower dates from about 1750. The mills produced flour until 1735, when the owners became involved in gin manufacture and called themselves

Three Mills: there has been a mill here since Saxon times

'millers and malt distillers'. Nicholson's Gin purchased the mills in 1872 and produced spirits here until 1952. Hedges and Butler used Clock Mill as a bonded warehouse. As early as 1588 there had been a brief attempt at making gun-powder, and in 1916 the biochemist and future first president of Israel, Dr Chaim Weizmann, worked in the Clock Mill producing ace-tone, a solvent for making cordite. The House Mill is open May–Oct Sun 2–4pm; admission charge.

The Victorian bottling plant, at the far end of the cobbled street, is now a film studio. In the *London Bridge* television soap Three Mills was used for the Bermondsey scenes. Other television series made here include *Kavanagh QC* and *Big Brother*.

Walk up Three Mill Lane to pass Tesco (left). Turn left and beyond a side turning join the main road which rises to cross the railway. Bromley-by-Bow Station is on far side of the road.

To reach Bromley-by-Bow Station: At the top of the railway bridge go left down steps and under the dual carriageway to the station entrance.

Refreshments

Three Mills: Tesco, Three Mill Lane; sandwiches and coffee machine; open 24 hours Mon 8am–Sat 10pm, and Sun 10am–4pm.

Three Mills: The Still Café, Three Mills Studios; tel. 020 8215 0125.

18. Bromley-by-Bow to Canning Town

*Bromley-by-Bow Station (London Underground District line)
to Canning Town (London Underground Jubilee line, DLR and
Silverlink Metro)*

Maps:	19–20
Distance:	1¼ miles (2km)
OS Map:	**OS Explorer 162 (Greenwich and Gravesend)**

The River Lea is lost for much of this section as the navigation
turns south-west away from the Lea and the Walk heads east to
cross the Meridian Line. At Canning Town the river reappears as
the natural, winding, tidal Lea. Whilst access to the gasworks site
remains limited it will sometimes be necessary to reach Canning
Town by way of the underground, changing at West Ham.

BROMLEY-BY-BOW is the south side of Bow. *Bromley-by-
Bow* means *bramble-covered wood beside Bow*. Until 1968 the
station, which opened in 1858, was confusingly called just
Bromley. Old Palace School in St Leonard's Street is a
reminder that James I is said to have stayed at a house on
the site – the Victoria and Albert Museum has one of the
rooms. Twelvetrees Crescent is named after a 19th-century
soap manufacturer.

To reach the Walk from Bromley-by-Bow Station: Turn left to go
down steps and under the main road. On the far side turn left.

Walk along the main road with traffic to the right. Turn left
into Twelvetrees Crescent and keep ahead through the gateway.
The road crosses the river to run by the Bromley-by-Bow
gasworks.

BROMLEY-BY-BOW GASWORKS is the site of a rocket
factory founded in 1809 by William Congreve, who invented
the Congreve Rocket and experimented with gas. He rented

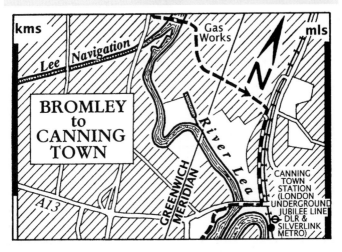

MAP 20

riverside Westham Abbey pasture between the railway and Twelvetrees Crescent Bridges in about 1821, and after his death it continued to be used for rocket research until 1862. The Imperial Gas Company began building its gasworks here in 1870. Gas production was run down in the early 1960s, leaving seven of the eight Victorian gas holders which are now used for storing natural gas.

Go right at a junction by Dudley's huge warehouse. To the left are memorials to gas workers who died in the two world wars. Pass through more security gates and the main gates round the corner to enter Cody Road.

Walk ahead to cross the Greenwich Meridian Line, which runs down the middle of South Crescent (first right turning). Continue down Cody Road to pass the sandwich bar at the far end. Go right into Stephenson Street and, well before the Dartmouth Arms, turn left and right across a redundant level crossing. Follow the road alongside the Jubilee line (left).

Keep ahead, passing the Turkish baths and the Durham Arms, to the main road by the Bridge House Hotel. Turn left, and just before the main junction go right to cross the dual carriageway, passing under the flyover. (Turn right for the final section.)

To reach Canning Town Station: Bear left for the bus stops and station.

Refreshments
Cody Road: Nibbles Sandwich Bar, Cody Road; Mon–Fri 8am–3pm.

Accommodation
Contact Tower Hamlets TIC, tel. 020 7375 2549.

19. Canning Town to East India Dock

Canning Town (London Underground Jubilee Line, DLR and Silverlink Metro) to East India Dock Station (DLR)

Maps:	**20–21**
Distance:	**1 mile (1.5km)**
OS Map:	**OS Explorer 162 (Greenwich and Gravesend)**

From Canning Town the Walk is alongside the River Lea's winding tidal Bow Creek to reach the Lea Valley Walk's climax opposite the Thames-side Millennium Dome.

CANNING TOWN The name can be traced back to 1851, although its origin is uncertain. It is said to be named after Lord Canning, governor-general of India, who had links with this area through the docks. However, it may come from a local industry or the name of an employer. The area was briefly known as Hallsville after the landlord Mr Hall. There is still a Hallsville road, school and pub. The landmark St Luke's Church, with its continental spire, was completed in 1876 and has recently been converted into a health and community centre with four new floors added. Outside there is often a pleasant aroma from Goswell's bakery. The more famous church here is the Mayflower Church, rebuilt in 1930 as part of Vincent Street's Mayflower Family Centre, founded in 1894. Two years earlier Keir Hardy had become the member of parliament and first Labour MP.

To reach the Walk: Leave the station by the north exit and bear half-left to East India Dock Road.

Walk along the main East India Dock Road. The river is over to the left. After a short distance turn left off the road onto a path leading to the waterside. Stay with the river until it begins to swing north with the sharp river bend. The path turns inland by silos.

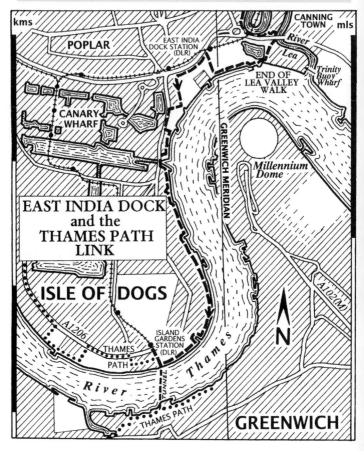

MAP 21

Turn left along Orchard Place, but before entering Pura Foods, which occupies the peninsula, go right along a narrow passage leading to the river. This view is the last glimpse of the Lea before its confluence with the Thames. The green left bank was once the

Thames Ironworks, with a wet dock and downstream slipways beyond.

THAMES IRONWORKS The Thames Ironworks and Shipbuilding Company opened in 1846. Warships for Japan, Russia and many European countries as well as Britain were built here. HMS 'Warrior', now at Portsmouth, was launched in 1860. Ironwork for Hammersmith, Blackfriars Railway and Westminster bridges was manufactured here, and many early RNLI lifeboats were also built. The works football club, founded in 1900, is now West Ham Football Club and still known as the Hammers after riveters' hammers. The works closed in 1912 after the launch of HMS 'Thunderer'.

After a short distance the path passes under the new Lower Lea Crossing flyover before returning to Orchard Place. Opposite is East India Dock and the end of the Walk.

ORCHARD PLACE There was once an orchard here, and the attached house was where the path turns inland from the river. The road leads directly to Trinity Buoy Wharf at the confluence of the Lea and Thames. The site, with water on three sides, was owned by Trinity House from 1803 until 1988 and includes a lighthouse where Michael Faraday developed electric lighting for lighthouses. The wharf's name recalls the testing and repairing of iron buoys which took place here from 1869. The 180ft long chain- and cable-proving house is now used for exhibitions and special events whilst other buildings house artists studios. The wharf is open during daylight hours, but requests to visit the lighthouse should be made in advance (tel. 020 7515 7153).

Trinity Buoy Wharf is along the road to the left but the Walk continues ahead. Cross Orchard Place to go ahead through gates into East India Dock Basin. Once by the dock bear left to the viewpoint and Lea Valley Walk climax next to the lock gates.

EAST INDIA DOCK, now part of the Lee Valley Regional Park and the end of the Lea Valley Walk, was built between 1803 and 1806 for the East India Company to provide deep moorings for large ships. The 8 acre dock closed in 1967 and was mostly infilled, leaving the Entrance Basin. The view is of the Millennium Dome.

To reach East India Station: Turn right over the lock gates and follow the Thames upstream and along the front of Virginia Quay. At the far end go right inland along the line of the Meridian, crossing two roads, to the station.

Accommodation

Contact Tower Hamlets TIC, tel. 020 7375 2549.

20. Thames Path Link: East India Dock to Island Gardens

East India Dock Station (DLR) to Island Gardens (DLR)

Map:	**21**
Distance:	**3 miles (4.8km)**
OS Map:	**OS Explorer 162 (Greenwich and Gravesend)**

This 3 mile extension down the east side of the Isle of Dogs (open 2001) links the Lea Valley Walk to the Thames Path. On the way the riverside path crosses the Meridian.

EAST INDIA DOCK: see Walk 19.

From the East India Dock viewpoint, at the climax of the Lea Valley Walk, turn upstream over the East India Dock lock gates and follow the Thames riverside (left). Enter the gates of Virginia Quay.

  VIRGINIA QUAY, formerly Brunswick Wharf, is a housing development started in 1998 and named after the founders of Virginia, who embarked here in 1606. Names on the large memorial include John Smith, who was rescued by Princess Pocahontas from capture. In 1840 this was the terminus for the London and Blackwall Railway running out of Fenchurch Street. There was a hotel here for passengers transferring to steamers. After wartime bombing the site was extended by infilling part of the East India Export Dock to build a power station, which was demolished in 1989.

At the far end cross the Meridian Line and turn inland to the parallel road which passes behind the Reuters Docklands Centre.

  REUTERS DOCKLANDS CENTRE The black building, by Richard Rogers and opened in 1989, has a satellite system on the roof. Reuters gathers and supplies news and business information 24 hours a day worldwide.

On turning south (by Majestic Wine and the Ibis Hotel) the road becomes Blackwall Way. At the White Swan go right along Yabsley Street to avoid Northumberland Wharf rubbish transfer station. At the main Prestons Road go left. After crossing onto the Isle of Dogs at the former Blackwall Basin entrance go left into Coldharbour on the north-east corner of the Isle of Dogs.

ISLE OF DOGS, known as Stepney Marsh until Henry VIII had his kennels built there, was called an island before becoming a real island in 1805, when West India Dock was given an eastern entrance. Today's landmark is the 50-storey Canary Wharf Tower, Britain's tallest building, completed in 1991. Occupiers include the *Independent, Mirror* and *Telegraph* newspapers.

COLDHARBOUR was a causeway from Blackwall, with houses here from as early as the 1680s. Isle House was a dockmaster's residence built in 1825 by Sir John Rennie, son of John Rennie the elder. The Gun pub, dating from about 1710, is said to have been a meeting place for Lord Nelson and Lady Hamilton.

In Coldharbour the view is hidden by the row of riverside houses. At The Gun turn back to the main road to cross the lifting Blue Bridge over the West India Docks entrance.

BLUE BRIDGE was erected in the 1980s during the Docklands' regeneration.

At once go left along the back of the Pierhead to the river and past the Pierhead Lock development. Soon there is the Storm Water Pumping Station.

STORM WATER PUMPING STATION, designed by John Outram and completed in 1988, with its flying Chinese-style eaves, is one of Docklands' outstanding new buildings. The blue bricks represent the river.

The path is briefly inland to avoid the riverside gardens, but soon it is necessary to return to the main road for a few yards due to a long fence at Riverbarge Close. Beyond the Samuda Estate tower block is the London Yard inlet.

LONDON YARD was built during 1980–1984 by Dutch developers – hence the street names behind. The 25-storey tower block to the north was built in 1957 as GLC housing. Millwall Wharf to the south, redeveloped in the late 1990s, includes the 1901 sugar warehouses.

Walk along Millwall Wharf (open 2001) to Compass Point.

COMPASS POINT, formerly Dudgeon's Wharf, is now a housing estate designed by Jeremy Dixon and completed in 1988. Along the riverside are paired town houses with now mature gardens and an inland streetscape imitating Brighton and Kensington.

At Cubitt Wharf the path runs behind the building.

CUBITT WHARF, formerly Cubitt Town Wharf, was part of Cubitt Town, which covered a mile of river frontage on the south-east corner of the Isle of Dogs. It was developed in the 1840s and 1850s by William Cubitt, brother of Thomas and Lewis, who built Belgravia (see 'Newcastle Draw Dock', below).

The riverside path is now along Saunders Ness, which leads to Newcastle Draw Dock in front of the Watermans Arms.

NEWCASTLE DRAW DOCK was built about 1850 and used for transferring cargo from coasters and barges to carts. This was part of Cubitt Town, with the Waterman's Arms, Christ Church and its vicarage all added by 1860. The residential Cumberland Mills, on the dock's west side, was completed in 1987 on the site of an 1850 oil seed mill.

Continue past Cumberland Mills and Luralda Wharf to enter Island Gardens and join the Thames Path at the far end.

ISLAND GARDENS was created at the end of the 19th century by the Royal Naval College opposite to improve their view. Once this southern tip of the Isle of Dogs was reed

The Royal Observatory at Greenwich

beds and here, in about 1750, Canaletto studied the view for his painting *Greenwich Palace*.

From here westwards upstream the Thames Path runs as a dual route along both banks of the Thames as far as Teddington. At Island Gardens, therefore, the Thames Path runs both west round the Isle of Dogs as well as through the foot tunnel to Greenwich. Thames Path guidebooks are on sale at the Greenwich Tourist Information Centre, near the 'Cutty Sark'.

GREENWICH is home to the former Royal Naval College. Wren's impressive buildings are now part of the National Maritime Museum, as is the Observatory on the hill, through which the Greenwich Meridian Line passes. The 'Cutty Sark' tea clipper stands below in dry dock.

To reach Island Gardens Station: Leave Island Gardens by the gate opposite the tunnel.

Refreshments

Coldharbour: The Gun; open all day.

Island Gardens: Café; open all day most days.

Accommodation

Contact Greenwich TIC, tel. 0870 608 2000.

BIBLIOGRAPHY

Hatts, Leigh: *Country Walks Around London* (David & Charles, 1983)

Hinde, Thomas: *The Domesday Book: England's Heritage Then and Now* (Hutchinson, 1985)

Houfe, Simon: *Bedfordshire* (Pimlico, 1995)

Jenkins, Simon: *England's Thousand Best Churches* (Penguin, 1999)

Lewis, Jim: *London's Lea Valley* (Phillimore, 1999)

Pevsner, Nikolaus: *The Buildings of England* county series (Penguin)

Thomas, Richard: *A Guide to the Lee and Stort Navigations* (Lea and Stort Planning Amenities Forum, 1994)

Weinreb, Ben and Hibbert, Christopher: *The London Encyclopaedia* (Macmillan, 1983)

Dockland: Historical Survey (NELP/GLC, 1986)

OS Guide to Waterways (Nicholson, 1989)

CICERONE GUIDES

SOUTH AND SOUTH-WEST Long-distance trails

THE KENNET & AVON WALK
THE SOUTHERN COAST-TO-COAST WALK
SOUTH WEST WAY - A Walker's Guide to the Coast Path (2 Volumes)
THE THAMES PATH
THE TWO MOORS WAY
THE WEALDWAY AND THE VANGUARD WAY
SOUTHERN AND SOUTH-EAST ENGLAND
CANAL WALKS Vol 3: South
CHANNEL ISLAND WALKS
WALKING IN THE CHILTERNS
A WALKER'S GUIDE TO THE ISLE OF WIGHT
WALKING IN KENT (2 volumes)
LONDON THEME WALKS
RURAL RIDES No.1: WEST SURREY
RURAL RIDES No.2: EAST SURREY
WALKING IN SUSSEX
WALKING IN BUCKINGHAMSHIRE
WALKING IN BEDFORDSHIRE
WALKING IN HAMPSHIRE

SOUTH AND SOUTH-WEST

CORNISH ROCK
WALKING IN CORNWALL
WALKING ON DARTMOOR
WALKING IN DEVON
WALKING IN DORSET
A WALKER'S GUIDE TO THE PUBS OF DARTMOOR
EXMOOR AND THE QUANTOCKS
WALKING IN SOMERSET
WALKING IN THE ISLES OF SCILLY

LONG DISTANCE TRAILS ACROSS NORTHERN ENGLAND

WALKING THE CLEVELAND WAY AND THE MISSING LINK
THE DALES WAY
THE ISLE OF MAN COASTAL PATH
THE ALTERNATIVE PENNINE WAY
THE PENNINE WAY
LAUGHS ALONG THE PENNINE WAY
THE ALTERNATIVE COAST TO COAST
A NORTHERN COAST TO COAST

LAKE DISTRICT and MORECAMBE BAY

CONISTON COPPER MINES: A Field Guide

CICERONE GUIDES

THE CUMBRIA WAY AND ALLERDALE RAMBLE
THE EDEN WAY
THE ISLE OF MAN COASTAL PATH
A LAKE DISTRICT ANGLER'S GUIDE
SHORT WALKS IN LAKELAND
Book 1: SOUTH LAKELAND
Book 2: NORTH LAKELAND
Book 3: WEST LAKELAND
SCRAMBLES IN THE LAKE DISTRICT
MORE SCRAMBLES IN THE LAKE DISTRICT
THE TARNS OF LAKELAND VOL I: WEST
THE TARNS OF LAKELAND VOL 2: EAST
WALKING ROUND THE LAKES
WALKS IN THE SILVERDALE/ARNSIDE AONB
WINTER CLIMBS IN THE LAKE DISTRICT

NORTH-WEST ENGLAND outside the Lake District
WALKING IN CHESHIRE
FAMILY WALKS IN THE FOREST OF BOWLAND
WALKING IN THE FOREST OF BOWLAND
CANAL WALKS, Vol 1: North
LANCASTER CANAL WALKS
A WALKER'S GUIDE TO THE LANCASTER CANAL
WALKS FROM THE LEEDS-LIVERPOOL CANAL
THE RIBBLE WAY
WALKS IN RIBBLE COUNTRY
WALKING IN LANCASHIRE
WALKS ON THE WEST PENNINE MOORS
WALKS IN LANCASHIRE WITCH COUNTRY

PENNINES AND NORTH-EAST ENGLAND
CANOEISTS' GUIDE TO THE NORTH-EAST
HADRIAN'S WALL Vol 1: The wall walk
HADRIAN'S WALL Vol 2:
NORTH YORKS MOORS
THE REIVER'S WAY
THE TEESDALE WAY
WALKING IN COUNTY DURHAM
WALKING IN THE NORTH PENNINES
WALKING IN NORTHUMBERLAND
WALKING IN THE SOUTH
WALKING IN THE WOLDS
WALKS IN THE NORTH YORK MOORS Book 1
WALKS IN THE NORTH YORK MOORS Book 2

CICERONE GUIDES

WALKS IN THE YORKSHIRE DALES - Book 1
WALKS IN THE YORKSHIRE DALES - Book 2
WALKS IN THE YORKSHIRE DALES - Book 3
WATERFALL WALKS - TEESDALE AND THE HIGH PENNINES
THE YORKSHIRE DALES
THE YORKSHIRE DALES ANGLER'S GUIDE

DERBYSHIRE PEAK DISTRICT and EAST MIDLANDS
"Star" FAMILY WALKS IN THE PEAK DISTRICT AND SOUTH YORKSHIRE
HIGH PEAK WALKS
WHITE PEAK WALKS Vol 1: THE NORTHERN DALES
WHITE PEAK WALKS Vol 2: THE SOUTHERN DALES
WHITE PEAK WAY
WEEKEND WALKS IN THE PEAK DISTRICT
WALKING IN SHERWOOD FOREST & THE DUKERIES
THE VIKING WAY

WALES, and WELSH BORDER Long-distance tßrails
THE LLEYN PENINSULA COASTAL PATH
WALKING OFFA'S DYKE PATH
OWAIN GLYNDWR'S WAY
THE PEMBROKESHIRE COASTAL PATH
SARN HELEN
THE SHROPSHIRE WAY
WALKING DOWN THE WYE
A WELSH COAST TO COAST WALK

WALES, AND WELSH BORDERS
ASCENT OF SNOWDON
ANGLESEY COAST WALKS
THE BRECON BEACONS
CLWYD ROCK
HEREFORD AND THE WYE VALLEY
HILL WALKING IN SNOWDONIA
HILLWALKING IN WALES (2 Volumes)
THE MOUNTAINS OF ENGLAND AND WALES Vol 1: WALES
THE RIDGES OF SNOWDONIA
SCRAMBLES IN SNOWDONIA
SEVERN WALKS
THE SHROPSHIRE HILLS
SNOWDONIA WHITE WATER, SEA AND SURF
SPIRIT PATHS OF WALES
WELSH WINTER CLIMBS THE MIDLANDS
CANAL WALKS Vol: 2 Midlands

CICERONE GUIDES

THE COTSWOLD WAY
COTSWOLD WALKS (3 volumes)
THE GRAND UNION CANAL WALK
AN OXBRIDGE WALK
WALKING IN OXFORDSHIRE
WALKING IN WARWICKSHIRE
WALKING IN WORCESTERSHIRE
WEST MIDLANDS ROCK

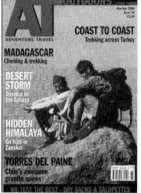